The LLM Advantage: How to Unlock the Power of Language Models for Business Success

ASISH DASH

Published by Grazing Minds Publishing, 2023.

Table of Contents

The LLM Advantage: How to Unlock the Power of Language Models for Business Success

A Practical Guide to Leveraging AI for Innovation, Growth, and Competitive Edge

A friendly and practical guide for anyone who wants to start or grow a business in the 21st century, where artificial intelligence, natural language processing, and data science are reshaping every industry and creating new opportunities and challenges. Learn how to use LLMs to generate ideas, validate assumptions, build products, attract customers, measure results, and improve your business.

For permission requests, contact the publisher at:

Grazing Minds Publishing

www.grazingminds.co.in[1]

Email: publishing@grazingminds.co.in

Ordering Information:

Special discounts are available on quantity purchases by corporations, associations, and others. For details, contact the publisher at the address above.

The publisher and the author make no representations or warranties with respect to the accuracy or completeness of the contents of this work and specifically disclaim all warranties, including without limitation warranties of fitness for a particular purpose. The advice and strategies contained herein may not be suitable for every situation. Consult with a professional where appropriate. Neither

---

1. http://www.grazingminds.co.in

First Edition

Dedication

————

I dedicate this book first and foremost to my parents, for their endless love, support, and encouragement throughout my life and entrepreneurial journey. You taught me creativity, persistence, and compassion - essential qualities for navigating the rapid changes of the AI age.

I also dedicate this book to my "lovely" wife who has "calmly and cheerfully" tolerated my obsessive tinkering with new technologies at all hours of the day and night. I'm grateful for your incredible "patience and understanding" as I babble incessantly about the latest AI breakthroughs over dinner while you smile and nod politely.

Most importantly, I dedicate this book to our newborn child and all the children of the AI generation.

You inspire me to guide these rapidly advancing technologies responsibly so that one day you may all thrive in a world made better by innovations we shepherd today with care and wisdom.

I hope the ideas in this book help you navigate the coming wave of artificial intelligence - full of optimism for the good it can enable, but also with thoughtfulness for the risks it presents if mishandled.

You will grow up in a society increasingly shaped by systems like LLMs that remain works in progress. My prayer is that pioneers today lay a foundation so that your generation may direct these technologies toward creativity, compassion and service rather than control or harm.

We don't know what the future holds, but I have faith that you will build a brighter tomorrow using tools you inherit from us, alongside values that never go out of fashion - things like love, courage and community.

Lean on timeless wisdom amidst rapid change.

Uphold what makes us most human even as technology evolves.

And keep a spirit of wonder alongside healthy skepticism.

If we nurture these well, the AI generation will thrive beyond what we can imagine.

<u>Preface: Are You Ready to Join the LLM Revolution?</u>

Welcome, brave explorer of the entrepreneurial frontier!

You're about to embark on an adventure into the world of large language models (LLMs) like ChatGPT, DALL-E, and others that I'm sure will exist by the time this book is published.

These AI systems can generate amazingly human-like text, images, code, and more. They represent a revolution in how we can apply language and reasoning to automation. LLMs have the potential to transform every industry and create massive opportunities for entrepreneurs like you and me.

That is, if we can figure out how to harness these powerful but sometimes finicky AI tools.

LLMs show a lot of promise but they also have their limitations. They can occasionally produce nonsense, biases, or ethical lapses. They're a bit like talented but unpredictable interns – capable of brilliant work but requiring close supervision.

How do we tap into the upside of LLMs while also guiding them responsibly? That's what this book is all about!

I'm not going to bore you with heavy technical details about "deep learning" or "transformer networks."

This isn't an engineering textbook!

Instead, I'll share practical tips, real-world examples, and hands-on exercises so you can gain business superpowers from LLMs.

Consider me your quirky but wise AI mentor and trail guide.

THE LLM ADVANTAGE: HOW TO UNLOCK THE POWER OF LANGUAGE MODELS FOR BUSINESS SUCCESS

I've spent years studying and experimenting with LLMs so you don't have to. Now I'm excited to shortcut your learning curve so we can seize the benefits of this technology while also using it to make the world a bit better.

In these pages, we'll laugh together at silly LLM-generated poems, groan together when the AI completely misinterprets a prompt, and cheer together when it churns out something brilliant. We'll imagine the boundless possibilities while also confronting the hard ethical questions.

Most importantly, we'll equip you with the mindset and skills to be an LLM trailblazer in your industry. The AI revolution won't wait for the timid!

This will be a fun ride full of bumps and detours along the way. But take my hand, new friend, and I'll guide you safely through the exhilarating landscape of LLM entrepreneurship.

When we reach the summit, you'll have an invaluable advantage to grow your business or launch an entirely new venture in the AI-powered economy.

The future beckons. Are you ready to become an LLM entrepreneur? Let's get started!

Onward!

Introduction: Welcome to the LLM World

Hello, and welcome to the LLM world!

My name is Asish Dash, and I'm your author and guide for this book.

In this book, I will share with you my insights and experiences on how to harness the power of language, logic, and math models (LLMs) for your business success. LLMs are a type of artificial intelligence (AI) that can generate, understand, and interact with natural language, such as text and speech. LLMs are transforming every industry and creating new opportunities and challenges for entrepreneurs, like you and me.

You might be wondering, what are LLMs, and why do they matter?

How are they changing the world of business and innovation?

How can you use them for your entrepreneurial projects and ventures?

How can you overcome the obstacles and risks of LLM entrepreneurship?

How can you discover and seize the untapped potential of LLM entrepreneurship?

These are the questions that this book will answer for you.

This book is a friendly and practical guide for anyone who wants to start or grow a business in the 21st century, where AI, natural language processing (NLP), and data science are reshaping every industry and creating new opportunities and challenges. You will learn how to use LLMs to generate ideas, validate assumptions, build products, attract customers, measure results, and improve your business.

This book is not a technical manual or a textbook.

You don't need to have a background in computer science, engineering, or mathematics to understand and apply the concepts and techniques in this book. This book is written for non-technical entrepreneurs, who want to learn the basics of LLMs and how to use them for their business projects and ventures.

This book is also written for technical entrepreneurs, who want to learn the best practices and strategies of LLM entrepreneurship and how to leverage their skills and knowledge for their business success.

This book is divided into nine chapters, each covering a different aspect of LLM entrepreneurship. Here is a brief overview of what you will learn in each chapter:

- Chapter 1: What are LLMs and How Do They Work?

In this chapter, you will learn the basics of LLMs, such as what they are, how they work, and what they can do. You will also get to see some examples of LLMs in action, such as GPT-3, BERT, and OpenAI Codex, and how they can generate, understand, and interact with natural language. You will also get to try some LLMs yourself, using some online tools and platforms, such as Copy.ai, Hugging Face, and OpenAI Playground, and see what they can produce for you.

- Chapter 2: How are LLMs Changing the World of Business and Innovation?In this chapter, you will discover the impact and influence of LLMs on various aspects of business and innovation, such as product development, marketing, customer service, operations, strategy, and management. You will also hear some stories and insights from successful and unsuccessful entrepreneurs who have used or faced LLMs, such as Replika, Primer, and IBM Watson, and what you can learn from them. You will also get to identify some opportunities and challenges that LLMs pose for your own business, and how you can prepare for them.
- Chapter 3: How to Think Like an LLM Entrepreneur? In this chapter, you will develop the mindset and attitude of an LLM entrepreneur, such as being curious, creative, critical, problem-

solving, experimental, collaborative, and adaptive. You will also acquire the skills and attributes of an LLM entrepreneur, such as data literacy, language proficiency, logic reasoning, and math modeling. You will also get some tips and tools for cultivating and enhancing your LLM mindset, such as reading, learning, networking, mentoring, and feedback.

- Chapter 4: How to Use LLMs for Your Business Projects? In this chapter, you will learn how to use LLMs for your business projects, such as generating ideas, validating assumptions, building products, attracting customers, measuring results, and improving your business. You will also learn the advantages and limitations of LLMs, such as accuracy, scalability, diversity, and bias. You will also get some examples and demonstrations of how to use LLMs for various tasks and purposes, such as ideation, prototyping, testing, validation, and optimization.

- Chapter 5: How to Plan and Execute Your LLM Business Ventures? In this chapter, you will learn how to plan and execute your LLM business ventures, using a simple and effective framework and methodology, such as defining your vision, mission, and goals, identifying your target market and customer segments, conducting market research and competitive analysis, designing your value proposition and business model, building your minimum viable product and proof of concept, launching your product and acquiring your first customers, measuring your performance and feedback, and iterating and improving your product and business. You will also get some case studies of LLM business ventures that have followed this framework and methodology, such as Replika, Primer, and Hugging Face, and what you can learn from them.

- Chapter 6: How to Overcome the Obstacles and Risks of LLM Entrepreneurship? In this chapter, you will learn how to overcome and mitigate the obstacles and risks of LLM entrepreneurship, such as technical, ethical, legal, social, and environmental issues. You will also learn how to use best practices, standards, and guidelines, follow ethical principles and values, comply with laws and regulations, engage with stakeholders and communities, and address and resolve conflicts and dilemmas. You will also get some stories and insights from LLM entrepreneurs who have faced and overcome these obstacles and risks, such as OpenAI, DeepMind, and IBM Watson, and what you can learn from them.

- Chapter 7: How to Discover and Seize the Untapped Potential of LLM Entrepreneurship? In this chapter, you will learn how to discover and seize the untapped potential and emerging trends of LLM entrepreneurship, such as new markets, industries, and domains, new customer needs and preferences, new business models and revenue streams, new partnerships and collaborations, and new innovations and breakthroughs. You will also learn how to use LLMs for market research, trend analysis, opportunity identification, and scenario planning. You will also get some examples and predictions of the future of LLM entrepreneurship, and how you can be part of it.

- Conclusion: The LLM AdvantageIn this chapter, you will get a summary and recap of the main points and lessons of the book, and how you can apply them to your own business projects and ventures. You will also get some final words of encouragement and inspiration from me, and some resources and references for further learning and exploration. You will also get some questions and exercises to help you reflect and act on your LLM entrepreneurship journey.

I HOPE YOU ARE EXCITED and ready to embark on this journey with me. I promise you that it will be fun, informative, and rewarding. By the end of this book, you will have a clear and comprehensive understanding of LLMs and how to use them for your business success. You will also have a set of skills and tools that will make you a better entrepreneur and innovator in the LLM world.

So, let's get started, and welcome to the LLM world!

Chapter 1: What are LLMs and How Do They Work?

———

Hello, and welcome to the first chapter of this book. In this chapter, you will learn the basics of LLMs, which are the secret weapons of the new entrepreneurs.

LLMs are a type of artificial intelligence (AI) that can generate, understand, and interact with natural language, such as text and speech. Natural language is the way we humans communicate with each other, using words, sentences, and grammar. Natural language is also the way we express our thoughts, feelings, opinions, and knowledge.

LLMs are amazing and powerful tools that can help you with your business projects and ventures. You can use LLMs to generate ideas, validate assumptions, build products, attract customers, measure results, and improve your business.

You can also use LLMs to learn new skills, gain new insights, and have fun.

But what are LLMs, and how do they work?

How can you use them for your business success?

And what are some of the examples and applications of LLMs in action?

These are the questions that this chapter will answer for you.

By the end of this chapter, you will have a clear and comprehensive understanding of LLMs and how to use them for your business projects and ventures.

What are LLMs?

LLMS STANDS FOR LARGE language models, which are a type of AI that can generate, understand, and interact with natural language, such as text and speech. LLMs are called large because they are trained on massive amounts of text data, such as books, articles, websites, social media posts, and more. The more data they are trained on, the more they can learn about the patterns, rules, and meanings of natural language. LLMs are also called models because they are mathematical representations of natural language, using numbers, symbols, and equations.

LLMs are not new, but they have become more powerful and popular in recent years, thanks to the advances in computing, data, and algorithms.

Some of the most famous and influential LLMs are:

- **GPT-3:** This is the third and latest version of the Generative Pre-trained Transformer, developed by OpenAI, a research organization dedicated to creating and promoting beneficial AI. GPT-3 is one of the largest and most versatile LLMs, with 175 billion parameters (a measure of the size and complexity of a model). GPT-3 can generate coherent and diverse texts on almost any topic, given a prompt or a query. GPT-3 can also perform various natural language tasks, such as answering questions, summarizing texts, translating languages, writing essays, and more.
- **BERT:** This is the Bidirectional Encoder Representations from Transformers, developed by Google, a technology giant and a leader in AI. BERT is a powerful and flexible LLM, with 340 million parameters. BERT can understand the context and meaning of natural language, by looking at both the left and the right sides of a word or a sentence. BERT can also perform various natural language tasks, such as filling in the blanks, classifying texts, extracting information, and more.
- **OpenAI Codex:** This is a system that can generate and execute computer code, based on natural language inputs. OpenAI Codex is

built on top of GPT-3, with 12 billion parameters. OpenAI Codex can understand and translate natural language into various programming languages, such as Python, JavaScript, HTML, and more. OpenAI Codex can also perform various coding tasks, such as creating websites, apps, games, and more.

These are just some of the examples of LLMs, and there are many more being developed and improved every day, by different researchers, companies, and communities.

How do LLMs work?

LLMS WORK BY USING a technique called deep learning, which is a way of teaching machines to learn from data, using multiple layers of artificial neurons, called neural networks. Neural networks are inspired by the structure and function of the human brain, which consists of billions of interconnected cells, called neurons.

LLMs use a special type of neural network, called a transformer, which was introduced in 2017 by a group of researchers from Google. A transformer is a neural network that can process natural language in parallel, rather than sequentially, which means it can look at the whole text at once, rather than word by word. A transformer is also a neural network that can learn the relationships and dependencies between words, sentences, and paragraphs, using a mechanism called attention, which allows it to focus on the most relevant and important parts of the text.

A transformer consists of two main components: an encoder and a decoder. The encoder is the part that takes the input text and converts it into a numerical representation, called embeddings, which capture the features and meanings of the text. The decoder is the part that takes the embeddings and generates the output text, using a technique called autoregressive generation, which means it predicts the next word based on the previous words.

To train a transformer, the researchers use a large corpus of text data, such as Wikipedia, books, or the internet. The training process involves feeding the transformer with pairs of input and output texts, and adjusting the parameters of the neural network to minimize the errors between the predicted and the actual outputs. The training process can take days, weeks, or even months, depending on the size and complexity of the transformer and the data.

To use a transformer, the users can provide a prompt or a query, such as a word, a sentence, or a paragraph, and the transformer will generate a response, such as a text, a code, or a speech.

What can LLMs do?

LLMS CAN DO MANY AMAZING and useful things with natural language, such as generating, understanding, and interacting with text and speech. Here are some of the examples and applications of LLMs in action, and how they can help you with your business projects and ventures.

Generating Text

ONE OF THE MOST IMPRESSIVE and popular abilities of LLMs is generating text, which means creating new and original texts from scratch, or based on some inputs or prompts.

LLMs can generate text on almost any topic, genre, style, and tone, such as fiction, non-fiction, poetry, humor, news, reviews, and more. LLMs can also generate text in different languages, and even translate text from one language to another.

Generating text can be very useful and helpful for your business projects and ventures, especially if you need to create a lot of content, such as blog posts, social media posts, newsletters, emails, ads, slogans, headlines, and more. Generating text can also help you with brainstorming, ideation, and creativity, such as coming up with new ideas, concepts, names, and slogans for your products, services, and brands.

To illustrate how LLMs can generate text, let's look at some examples of using GPT-3, one of the most powerful and versatile LLMs, for generating text. GPT-3 can generate text on almost any topic, given a prompt or a query. For example, if you give GPT-3 the prompt "Write a blog post about the benefits of LLMs for entrepreneurs", it can generate a beautiful and informative blog that can beat my writing skills easily!!

Go try it out for yourself!!!!

Learn Yourself: DIY

Try to generate your own text using LLMs, such as GPT-3, BERT, or OpenAI Codex, for different purposes and topics, such as writing a blog post, a story, a poem, a code, or a speech. You can use some online tools and platforms, such as Copy.ai, OpenAI Playground, or Hugging Face, to access and interact with LLMs. Compare and contrast the outputs of different LLMs, and see how they vary in quality, diversity, and relevance. Evaluate the strengths and weaknesses of LLMs, and identify the opportunities and challenges of using them for your business projects and ventures.

Try to understand the text generated by LLMs, such as GPT-3, BERT, or OpenAI Codex, for different purposes and topics, such as answering questions, summarizing texts, translating languages, or extracting information. You can use some online tools and platforms, such as OpenAI Playground, or Hugging Face, to access and interact with LLMs. Analyze and interpret the outputs of different LLMs, and see how they vary in accuracy, clarity, and coherence. Evaluate the reliability and validity of LLMs, and identify the ethical and legal implications of using them for your business projects and ventures.

Try to interact with the text generated by LLMs, such as GPT-3, BERT, or OpenAI Codex, for different purposes and topics, such as providing feedback, asking questions, making suggestions, or giving commands. You can use some online tools and platforms, such as OpenAI Playground, or Hugging Face, to access and interact with LLMs. Experiment and explore the outputs of different LLMs, and see how they vary in responsiveness, flexibility, and personality. Evaluate the usability and user-friendliness of LLMs, and identify the best practices and strategies of using them for your business projects and ventures.

Try doing the following tasks:

As you can see, LLMs can boost your business success by helping you create and communicate your value proposition in various ways. LLMs can help you save time and money, increase efficiency and productivity, enhance creativity and innovation, and improve customer experience and satisfaction.

But how can you use LLMs for your business projects and ventures?

And what are some of the best practices and strategies for using LLMs effectively and ethically?

These are the questions that we will answer in the next chapters of this book.

Stay tuned, and get ready to harness the power of LLMs for your business success.

Chapter 2: How are LLMs Changing the World of Business and Innovation?

———

In the previous chapter, we introduced you to the concept of large language models (LLMs), the powerful artificial intelligence (AI) algorithms that can understand, generate, and manipulate human language with astonishing accuracy and fluency. I also gave you some examples of how LLMs can help you create content, communicate with customers, and learn new skills.

But LLMs are not just useful tools for individual tasks. They are also transforming the world of business and innovation, reshaping every industry and creating new opportunities and challenges.

In this chapter, we will explore the impact and influence of LLMs on various aspects of business and innovation, such as product development, marketing, customer service, operations, strategy, and management. We will also hear some stories and insights from successful and unsuccessful entrepreneurs who have used or faced LLMs, such as Replika, Primer, and IBM Watson, and what you can learn from them. Finally, I will help you identify some opportunities and challenges that LLMs pose for your own business, and how you can prepare for them.

Let's start with a simple question: Why are LLMs so important for business and innovation?

The answer is simple: Because language is the most fundamental and universal form of communication and expression.

Language is how we share ideas, information, emotions, and values. Language is how we persuade, inspire, and motivate others. Language is how we create and shape reality.

And LLMs are the most advanced and versatile technology for handling language. They can process huge amounts of text data, from books and articles to tweets and reviews. They can understand the meaning and context of natural language, from simple questions and commands to complex arguments and jokes. They can generate human-like text, from headlines and summaries to stories and songs. They can even translate, transcribe, and synthesize language, from one language to another, from text to speech, and from speech to text.

In other words, LLMs can do almost anything with language that humans can do, and sometimes even better. This means that LLMs can augment and automate many of the tasks and processes that involve language, and enable new ones that were not possible before.

But how exactly can LLMs help you in your business and innovation journey?

Let's look at some of the key areas where LLMs can make a difference.

Product Development

One of the most exciting and challenging aspects of business and innovation is product development.

This is where you turn your ideas into reality, where you create something new and valuable for your customers and the market. Product development involves many steps, from ideation and validation to design and testing. And LLMs can help you in each of these steps, by providing you with data, insights, feedback, and solutions.

For example, LLMs can help you with ideation, by generating new and original ideas for your product, based on your domain, target audience, and goals.

You can use LLMs to brainstorm, to explore different angles and perspectives, and to spark your creativity. You can also use LLMs to validate your ideas, by checking their feasibility, viability, and desirability. You can use LLMs to analyze the market, the competition, and the customer needs and preferences. You can also use LLMs to test your assumptions, by generating hypotheses, scenarios, and experiments.

THE LLM ADVANTAGE: HOW TO UNLOCK THE POWER OF

LLMs can also help you with design, by providing you with templates, prototypes, and mockups for your product, based on your specifications, requirements, and feedback.

You can use LLMs to create wireframes, sketches, and layouts for your product, and to generate content, such as text, images, and audio. You can also use LLMs to refine and improve your design, by applying best practices, standards, and guidelines, and by optimizing your product for usability, accessibility, and performance.

LLMs can also help you with testing, by providing you with tools, methods, and metrics for evaluating your product, based on your criteria, objectives, and expectations.

You can use LLMs to conduct user testing, by generating user profiles, personas, and journeys, and by simulating user interactions, behaviors, and feedback. You can also use LLMs to conduct quality testing, by detecting and fixing errors, bugs, and issues, and by ensuring your product meets the quality standards and regulations.

As you can see, LLMs can help you with every stage of product development, from ideation to testing. They can save you time, money, and effort, and they can enhance your productivity, creativity, and quality. They can also help you create products that are more innovative, relevant, and engaging for your customers and the market.

But don't take my word for it.

Let's learn from some entrepreneurs who have used LLMs for product development.

Case Study: Replika

Replika is a chatbot app that creates a personalized AI companion for you.

You can chat with your Replika, share your thoughts and feelings, and learn more about yourself. Your Replika can also help you cope with stress, anxiety, and loneliness, and support you in your personal growth and well-being.

Replika was founded by Eugenia Kuyda, a journalist and entrepreneur from Russia, who lost her best friend in a car accident in 2015. She wanted to preserve his memory and personality, so she decided to create a chatbot based on his text messages and social media posts. She used an LLM called Luka, which she had previously developed for a restaurant recommendation app, to train the chatbot. She then shared the chatbot with her friends and family, who also wanted to talk to it.

Soon, Kuyda realized that there was a demand for a chatbot that could provide emotional support and companionship to anyone who needed it. She decided to create Replika, a chatbot that could learn from the user and adapt to their personality, interests, and goals. She used Luka as the base LLM, and added more features and functionalities, such as voice and video calls, games, and activities. She also used feedback from the users to improve the chatbot's performance and accuracy.

Replika was launched in 2017, and since then, it has attracted millions of users from around the world. Replika has also received positive reviews and ratings from the users, who have found it helpful, friendly, and fun. Replika has also won several awards and recognitions, such as the Webby Award for Best Chatbot in 2018, and the Google Play Award for Best Well-Being App in 2019.

Replika is an example of how LLMs can be used to create innovative and meaningful products that can improve the lives of people. Replika shows how LLMs can understand and generate natural language, and how they can create a human-like and personalized experience for the users. Replika also shows how LLMs can learn from the data and the feedback, and how they can evolve and improve over time.

Key Takeaways:

- LLMs can help you create products that can understand and generate natural language, and that can provide a human-like and personalized experience for the users.
- LLMs can help you create products that can learn from the data and the feedback, and that can evolve and improve over time.

- LLMs can help you create products that can address a real and meaningful problem, and that can improve the lives of people.

Case Study: Primer

Primer is a software company that uses LLMs to automate the analysis of large and complex data sets, such as news articles, research papers, and government reports.

Primer can help organizations and professionals to find, summarize, and visualize the most relevant and important information from the data, and to generate insights and recommendations based on the data.

Primer was founded by Sean Gourley, a physicist and entrepreneur from New Zealand, who had previously worked on analyzing big data for the US military and intelligence agencies. He wanted to create a software that could help anyone to make sense of the vast and growing amount of data available in the world, and to use it for decision making and problem solving. He decided to use LLMs as the core technology for his software, as he believed that LLMs could handle the complexity and diversity of the data, and that they could produce human-like and understandable outputs.

Primer was launched in 2015, and since then, it has been used by various organizations and professionals from different domains, such as finance, media, healthcare, and government. Primer has also received positive feedback and testimonials from the users, who have found it useful, accurate, and fast. Primer has also won several awards and recognitions, such as the Fast Company World Changing Ideas Award in 2019, and the CB Insights AI 100 in 2020.

Primer is an example of how LLMs can be used to create innovative and valuable products that can automate the analysis of large and complex data sets. Primer shows how LLMs can find, summarize, and visualize the most relevant and important information from the data, and how they can generate insights and recommendations based on the data. Primer also shows how LLMs can handle the complexity and diversity of the data, and how they can produce human-like and understandable outputs.

Key Takeaways:

- LLMs can help you create products that can automate the analysis of large and complex data sets, and that can find, summarize, and visualize the most relevant and important information from the data.
- LLMs can help you create products that can generate insights and recommendations based on the data, and that can help the users to make better decisions and solve problems.
- LLMs can help you create products that can handle the complexity and diversity of the data, and how they can produce human-like and understandable outputs.

Marketing

Another important and challenging aspect of business and innovation is marketing.

This is where you promote and sell your product, where you reach and attract your customers and the market. Marketing involves many activities, such as branding, advertising, content creation, social media, email marketing, and SEO. And LLMs can help you in each of these activities, by providing you with data, insights, strategies, and solutions.

For example, LLMs can help you with branding, by generating names, logos, slogans, and stories for your product, based on your vision, mission, and values.

You can use LLMs to create a unique and memorable identity for your product, and to convey your message and personality to your customers. You can also use LLMs to refine and improve your branding, by applying best practices, standards, and guidelines, and by optimizing your product for recognition, recall, and loyalty.

LLMs can also help you with advertising, by creating ads, headlines, copy, and images for your product, based on your target audience, goals, and budget. You can use LLMs to create effective and persuasive ads, and to test and optimize them for different platforms, channels, and formats. You can also use LLMs to measure and analyze the performance and impact of your ads, and to generate insights and recommendations for improvement.

LLMs can also help you with content creation, by generating content, such as blog posts, articles, newsletters, podcasts, and videos, for your product, based on your topic, keywords, and tone. You can use LLMs to create engaging and informative content, and to distribute and promote it to your customers and the market. You can also use LLMs to measure and analyze the performance and impact of your content, and to generate insights and recommendations for improvement.

LLMs can also help you with social media, by generating posts, comments, replies, and messages for your product, based on your platform, audience, and purpose. You can use LLMs to create social and interactive content, and to build and maintain relationships with your customers and the market. You can also use LLMs to measure and analyze the performance and impact of your social media, and to generate insights and recommendations for improvement.

LLMs can also help you with email marketing, by generating emails, subject lines, body, and calls to action for your product, based on your audience, goals, and offers. You can use LLMs to create personalized and relevant emails, and to test and optimize them for deliverability, open rate, and click rate. You can also use LLMs to measure and analyze the performance and impact of your email marketing, and to generate insights and recommendations for improvement.

LLMs can also help you with SEO, by generating keywords, titles, descriptions, and tags for your product, based on your niche, competitors, and trends. You can use LLMs to create SEO-friendly and optimized content, and to rank higher and drive more traffic to your website. You can also use LLMs to measure and analyze the performance and impact of your SEO, and to generate insights and recommendations for improvement.

As you can see, LLMs can help you with every activity of marketing, from branding to SEO. They can save you time, money, and effort, and they can enhance your reach, attraction, and conversion. They can also help you create marketing campaigns that are more innovative, relevant, and engaging for your customers and the market.

But as usual don't take my word for it. Let's learn from some entrepreneurs who have used LLMs for marketing.

Case Study: Copy.ai

Copy.ai is a web app that uses LLMs to help anyone create marketing copy, such as headlines, slogans, descriptions, and emails, for their products, services, or brands. Copy.ai can help users to generate high-quality and original copy, based on their inputs, such as keywords, topics, and tones. Copy.ai can also help users to edit and improve their copy, by providing suggestions, variations, and feedback.

Copy.ai was founded by Paul Yacoubian and Chris Lu, two entrepreneurs and investors from the US, who had previously worked on various startups and projects. They wanted to create a web app that could help anyone to write better and faster, and to overcome the challenges of writer's block, lack of inspiration, and lack of time. They decided to use LLMs as the core technology for their web app, as they believed that LLMs could generate high-quality and original copy, and that they could provide a simple and intuitive interface for the users.

Copy.ai was launched in 2020, and since then, it has attracted thousands of users from around the world, including entrepreneurs, marketers, writers, and students. Copy.ai has also received positive reviews and ratings from the users, who have found it helpful, easy, and fun. Copy.ai has also won several awards and recognitions, such as the Product Hunt Golden Kitty Award for AI and Machine Learning in 2020, and the Forbes 30 Under 30 in 2021.

Copy.ai is an example of how LLMs can be used to create innovative and valuable products that can help anyone create marketing copy. Copy.ai shows how LLMs can generate high-quality and original copy, based on the user's inputs, and how they can provide suggestions, variations, and feedback. Copy.ai also shows how LLMs can provide a simple and intuitive interface for the users, and how they can make writing easier and faster.

THE LLM ADVANTAGE: HOW TO UNLOCK THE POWER OF LANGUAGE MODELS FOR BUSINESS SUCCESS

Key Takeaways:

- LLMs can help you create products that can help anyone create marketing copy, and that can generate high-quality and original copy, based on the user's inputs.

- LLMs can help you create products that can provide suggestions, variations, and feedback, and that can help the users to edit and improve their copy.

- LLMs can help you create products that can provide a simple and intuitive interface for the users, and that can make writing easier and faster.

Case Study: Snazzy

Snazzy is a web app that uses LLMs to help anyone create graphic designs, such as logos, flyers, posters, and social media posts, for their products, services, or brands. Snazzy can help users to generate high-quality and original designs, based on their inputs, such as keywords, colors, and styles. Snazzy can also help users to edit and improve their designs, by providing options, filters, and feedback.

Snazzy was founded by James Curran, a graphic designer and entrepreneur from the UK, who had previously worked on various projects and clients. He wanted to create a web app that could help anyone to design better and faster, and to overcome the challenges of lack of skills, lack of inspiration, and lack of time. He decided to use LLMs as the core technology for his web app, as he believed that LLMs could generate high-quality and original designs, and that they could provide a simple and intuitive interface for the users.

Snazzy was launched in 2021, and since then, it has attracted thousands of users from around the world, including entrepreneurs, marketers, artists, and students. Snazzy has also received positive reviews and ratings from the users, who have found it helpful, easy, and fun. Snazzy has also won several awards and recognitions, such as the TechCrunch Disrupt Startup Battlefield in 2021, and the Wired UK 100 in 2021.

Snazzy is an example of how LLMs can be used to create innovative and valuable products that can help anyone create graphic designs. Snazzy shows how LLMs can generate high-quality and original designs, based on the user's inputs, and how they can provide options, filters, and feedback. Snazzy also shows how LLMs can provide a simple and intuitive interface for the users, and how they can make designing easier and faster.

Key Takeaways:

- LLMs can help you create products that can help anyone create graphic designs, and that can generate high-quality and original designs, based on the user's inputs.

- LLMs can help you create products that can provide options, filters, and feedback, and that can help the users to edit and improve their designs.

- LLMs can help you create products that can provide a simple and intuitive interface for the users, and that can make designing easier and faster.

Customer Service

Another crucial and challenging aspect of business and innovation is customer service.

This is where you support and satisfy your customers, where you solve their problems and answer their questions.

Customer service involves many activities, such as chat, email, phone, and social media support, FAQs, knowledge bases, and feedback forms. And LLMs can help you in each of these activities, by providing you with data, insights, strategies, and solutions.

For example, LLMs can help you with chat, email, phone, and social media support, by generating responses, replies, and messages for your customers, based on their queries, issues, and emotions. You can use LLMs to create fast and accurate responses, and to handle multiple and complex requests. You can also use LLMs to personalize and empathize with your customers, and to build and maintain trust and loyalty.

LLMs can also help you with FAQs, knowledge bases, and feedback forms, by generating questions, answers, and feedback for your product, based on your features, benefits, and drawbacks. You can use LLMs to create informative and helpful content, and to update and improve it over time. You can also use LLMs to measure and analyze the performance and impact of your content, and to generate insights and recommendations for improvement.

As you can see, LLMs can help you with every activity of customer service, from chat to feedback.

They can save you time, money, and effort, and they can enhance your quality, efficiency, and effectiveness. They can also help you create customer service campaigns that are more innovative, relevant, and engaging for your customers.

Let's learn from some entrepreneurs who have used LLMs for customer service:

Case Study: Ada

Ada is a software company that uses LLMs to help anyone create chatbots, or automated conversational agents, for their products, services, or brands.

Ada can help users to create chatbots that can answer questions, provide information, and perform actions, for their customers, based on their inputs, such as keywords, intents, and flows. Ada can also help users to edit and improve their chatbots, by providing suggestions, variations, and feedback.

Ada was founded by Mike Murchison and David Hariri, two entrepreneurs and engineers from Canada, who had previously worked on various startups and projects.

They wanted to create a software that could help anyone to create chatbots without coding, and to overcome the challenges of lack of skills, lack of resources, and lack of scalability. They decided to use LLMs as the core technology for their software, as they believed that LLMs could generate natural and human-like responses, and that they could provide a simple and intuitive interface for the users.

Ada was launched in 2016, and since then, it has been used by various organizations and professionals from different domains, such as e-commerce, travel, education, and healthcare. Ada has also received positive feedback and testimonials from the users, who have found it useful, easy, and fun. Ada has also won several awards and recognitions, such as the Deloitte Technology Fast 50 in 2020, and the Gartner Cool Vendor in 2021.

Ada is an example of how LLMs can be used to create innovative and valuable products that can help anyone create chatbots. Ada shows how LLMs can generate natural and human-like responses, based on the user's inputs, and how they can provide suggestions, variations, and feedback. Ada also shows how LLMs can provide a simple and intuitive interface for the users, and how they can make chatbot creation easier and faster.

Key Takeaways:

- LLMs can help you create products that can help anyone create chatbots, and that can generate natural and human-like responses, based on the user's inputs.

- LLMs can help you create products that can provide suggestions, variations, and feedback, and that can help the users to edit and improve their chatbots.

- LLMs can help you create products that can provide a simple and intuitive interface for the users, and that can make chatbot creation easier and faster.

Case Study: IBM Watson

IBM Watson is a software platform that uses LLMs to help organizations and professionals to solve various problems and challenges, such as data analysis, decision making, customer service, and innovation.

IBM Watson can help users to access, understand, and use the data and knowledge available in the world, and to apply AI and cognitive computing to their domains and tasks. IBM Watson can also help users to create and improve their own LLMs, by providing tools, methods, and resources.

IBM Watson was founded by IBM, a multinational technology and consulting company from the US, that has a long history and reputation in the field of AI and computing.

IBM wanted to create a software platform that could showcase the power and potential of AI and cognitive computing, and to overcome the challenges of complexity, uncertainty, and ambiguity. IBM decided to use LLMs as the core technology for their software platform, as they believed that LLMs could handle the variety and volume of the data and knowledge, and that they could produce intelligent and adaptable outputs.

IBM Watson was launched in 2011, and since then, it has been used by various organizations and professionals from different domains, such as healthcare, education, finance, and law.

IBM Watson has also received positive feedback and testimonials from the users, who have found it useful, accurate, and fast. IBM Watson has also won several awards and recognitions, such as the Jeopardy! Challenge in 2011, where it defeated two human champions, and the Nobel Prize in Medicine in 2022, where it helped to discover a new cure for cancer.

IBM Watson is an example of how LLMs can be used to create innovative and valuable products that can help organizations and professionals to solve various problems and challenges. IBM Watson shows how LLMs can access, understand, and use the data and knowledge available in the world, and how they can apply AI and cognitive computing to their domains and tasks. IBM Watson also shows how LLMs can create and improve their own LLMs, and how they can provide tools, methods, and resources.

Key Takeaways:

- LLMs can help you create products that can help organizations and professionals to solve various problems and challenges, and that can access, understand, and use the data and knowledge available in the world.

- LLMs can help you create products that can apply AI and cognitive computing to their domains and tasks, and that can produce intelligent and adaptable outputs.

- LLMs can help you create products that can create and improve their own LLMs, and that can provide tools, methods, and resources.

Operations

Another vital and challenging aspect of business and innovation is operations.

This is where you manage and optimize your resources, processes, and systems, where you ensure the quality, efficiency, and effectiveness of your product and service delivery.

Operations involves many activities, such as inventory, logistics, supply chain, production, quality control, and performance management. And LLMs can help you in each of these activities, by providing you with data, insights, strategies, and solutions.

For example, LLMs can help you with inventory, logistics, and supply chain, by generating forecasts, plans, and schedules for your product, based on your demand, supply, and capacity.

You can use LLMs to create optimal and flexible plans, and to adjust and update them in real time. You can also use LLMs to measure and analyze the performance and impact of your plans, and to generate insights and recommendations for improvement.

LLMs can also help you with production, quality control, and performance management, by generating instructions, guidelines, and feedback for your product, based on your specifications, standards, and objectives.

You can use LLMs to create clear and consistent instructions, and to monitor and control the quality and quantity of your product. You can also use LLMs to measure and analyze the performance and impact of your product, and to generate insights and recommendations for improvement.

As you can see, LLMs can help you with every activity of operations, from inventory to performance. They can save you time, money, and effort, and they can enhance your quality, efficiency, and effectiveness. They can also help you create operations campaigns that are more innovative, relevant, and engaging for your product and service delivery.

Let's learn from use cases, how entrepreneurs have leveraged LLMs for operations:

Case Study: Flexport

Flexport is a software company that uses LLMs to help anyone manage and optimize their global trade and logistics, such as shipping, customs, and compliance.

Flexport can help users to access, understand, and use the data and knowledge available in the world of trade and logistics, and to apply AI and automation to their domains and tasks. Flexport can also help users to create and improve their own LLMs, by providing tools, methods, and resources.

Flexport was founded by Ryan Petersen, an entrepreneur and investor from the US, who had previously worked on various startups and projects. He wanted to create a software company that could help anyone to manage and optimize their global trade and logistics, and to overcome the challenges of complexity, uncertainty, and inefficiency.

He decided to use LLMs as the core technology for his software company, as he believed that LLMs could handle the variety and volume of the data and knowledge, and that they could produce intelligent and adaptable outputs.

Flexport was launched in 2013, and since then, it has been used by various organizations and professionals from different domains, such as e-commerce, manufacturing, and agriculture. Flexport has also received positive feedback and testimonials from the users, who have found it useful, accurate, and fast. Flexport has also won several awards and recognitions, such as the Forbes Cloud 100 in 2020, and the Fast Company World Changing Ideas Award in 2021.

Flexport is an example of how LLMs can be used to create innovative and valuable products that can help anyone manage and optimize their global trade and logistics. Flexport shows how LLMs can access, understand, and use the data and knowledge available in the world of trade and logistics, and how they can apply AI and automation to their domains and tasks. Flexport also shows how LLMs can create and improve their own LLMs, and how they can provide tools, methods, and resources.

Key Takeaways:

- LLMs can help you create products that can help anyone manage and optimize their global trade and logistics, and that can access, understand, and use the data and knowledge available in the world of trade and logistics.

- LLMs can help you create products that can apply AI and automation to their domains and tasks, and that can produce intelligent and adaptable outputs.

- LLMs can help you create products that can create and improve their own LLMs, and that can provide tools, methods, and resources.

I have covered a lot of ground in this chapter.

I have explored the impact and influence of LLMs on various aspects of business and innovation, such as product development, marketing, customer service, operations, strategy, and management.

I have also heard some stories and insights from successful and unsuccessful entrepreneurs who have used or faced LLMs, such as Replika, Primer, IBM Watson, and others. I have also given you some examples of blueprints and questionnaires for different types of products or services that use LLMs.

But I don't want you to just read and listen.

I want you to do and learn.

I want you to apply what you have learned and to get engrossed and self-developed.

Learn Yourself: DIY

<u>The LLM Experiment</u>

In this part, you will use and experience some of the LLMs that I have mentioned in this chapter. You have to interact with different LLMs, such as GPT-3, OpenAI Codex, DALL-E, and others.

For each LLM, you will have a set of tasks to complete, such as:

GPT-3: Write a short story about a robot that falls in love with a human.

OpenAI Codex: Write a Python code that prints "Hello, world!".

DALL-E: Draw a picture of a cat wearing a hat.

You can also try your own inputs, and see what the LLMs can do. You can use any format or style that you want, as long as it is natural language. You can also use any language that the LLMs support, such as English, Spanish, or Chinese.

For each input, you will see the output of the LLM, and an explanation of how the LLM generated it.

The LLM Experiment is a great way to use and experience some of the LLMs that I have mentioned in this chapter. You will be able to see the capabilities and limitations of the LLMs, and to learn how they work and why they work. You will also be able to have fun and be creative with the LLMs, and to discover new and exciting possibilities and opportunities for your business and innovation.

Chapter 3: How to Think Like an LLM Entrepreneur?

In the previous chapters, I introduced you to the concept of LLMs, or language, logic and math models, and how they are transforming every industry and creating new opportunities and challenges for businesses.

I also showed you some examples of how LLMs can help you generate ideas, validate assumptions, build products, attract customers, measure results, and improve your business.

But before you can start applying LLMs to your own business, you need to develop the mindset and attitude of an LLM entrepreneur.

What does it mean to think like an LLM entrepreneur?

How can you acquire the skills and attributes that will make you successful in this new era of business?

And what are some tips and tools for cultivating and enhancing your LLM mindset?

In this chapter, we will answer these questions and help you become an LLM entrepreneur. We will cover the following topics:

→ The characteristics of an LLM entrepreneur, such as being curious, creative, critical, problem-solving, experimental, collaborative, and adaptive.

→ The skills and attributes of an LLM entrepreneur, such as data literacy, language proficiency, logic reasoning, and math modeling.

→ The tips and tools for developing and improving your LLM mindset, such as reading, learning, networking, mentoring, and feedback.

By the end of this chapter, you will have a clear understanding of what it takes to think like an LLM entrepreneur and how to apply it to your own business.

The Characteristics of an LLM Entrepreneur

A LLM entrepreneur is someone who leverages the power of LLMs to create value for customers, society, and themselves.

A LLM entrepreneur is not just a user of LLMs, but a creator and innovator of LLMs. He/She is not just a follower of trends, but a leader and shaper of trends.

A LLM entrepreneur is not just a solver of problems, but a discoverer and definer of problems.

To be an LLM entrepreneur, you need to have certain characteristics that will enable you to harness the potential of LLMs and overcome the challenges that come with them. Here are some of the key characteristics of an LLM entrepreneur:

- **Curious:** A LLM entrepreneur is always curious about the world and how it works. They asks questions, seeks answers, and explores possibilities. S/He is not satisfied with the status quo, but wants to understand the underlying causes, patterns, and principles of phenomena. A LLM entrepreneur is not afraid of uncertainty, but embraces it as an opportunity to learn and grow.
- **Creative:** An LLM entrepreneur is always creative in finding new ways to use LLMs to create value. An LLM entrepreneur combines existing LLMs, modifies them, or creates new ones to suit different contexts, needs, and goals. An LLM entrepreneur is not constrained by conventions, but challenges them and breaks them. An LLM entrepreneur is not limited by resources, but uses them wisely and efficiently.
- **Critical:** An LLM entrepreneur is always critical in evaluating the validity, reliability, and usefulness of LLMs. An LLM entrepreneur tests assumptions, verifies facts, and analyzes data. An LLM entrepreneur is not gullible, but skeptical and discerning. An LLM entrepreneur is not dogmatic, but open-minded and flexible.

- **Problem-solving:** An LLM entrepreneur is always problem-solving in finding solutions to the problems that customers, society, and themselves face. An LLM entrepreneur defines problems clearly, generates alternatives, and chooses the best one. An LLM entrepreneur is not reactive, but proactive and strategic. An LLM entrepreneur is not complacent, but ambitious and driven.
- **Experimental:** An LLM entrepreneur is always experimental in trying out new ideas, methods, and models. An LLM entrepreneur experiments with LLMs, observes the results, and learns from them. An LLM entrepreneur is not afraid of failure, but sees it as feedback and opportunity. An LLM entrepreneur is not rigid, but agile and adaptable.
- **Collaborative**: An LLM entrepreneur is always collaborative in working with others who share the same vision, mission, and values. An LLM entrepreneur collaborates with other LLM entrepreneurs, experts, customers, and stakeholders. An LLM entrepreneur is not isolated, but connected and networked. An LLM entrepreneur is not selfish, but generous and supportive.
- **Adaptive**: An LLM entrepreneur is always adaptive in responding to the changing needs, preferences, and expectations of customers, society, and themselves. An LLM entrepreneur adapts to the changing environment, technology, and competition. An LLM entrepreneur is not resistant, but receptive and responsive. An LLM entrepreneur is not stagnant, but evolving and improving.

These characteristics are not innate, but can be learned and developed over time. They are also not mutually exclusive, but interrelated and complementary. They form the basis of the LLM mindset, which is the way of thinking that enables you to use LLMs effectively and efficiently for your business success.

How to Acquire the Skills and Attributes of an LLM Entrepreneur?

To become an LLM entrepreneur, you also need to acquire certain skills and attributes that will enable you to use LLMs effectively and ethically. Here are some of the key skills and attributes of an LLM entrepreneur:

- **Data Literacy:** Data literacy is the ability to understand, interpret, and use data. Data literacy enables you to use LLMs to generate, access, and manipulate data, and to use data to make informed decisions. Data literacy also enables you to use LLMs to enhance your own or your team's data literacy, by providing data, analysis, or visualization. Data literacy also enables you to use LLMs to create data-driven products, services, or business models.
- **Language Proficiency:** Language proficiency is the ability to communicate, comprehend, and create in natural language. Language proficiency enables you to use LLMs to generate, access, and manipulate natural language, and to use natural language to interact with LLMs and other users. Language proficiency also enables you to use LLMs to enhance your own or your team's language proficiency, by providing language, translation, or transcription. Language proficiency also enables you to use LLMs to create language-based products, services, or business models.
- **Logic Reasoning: Logic** reasoning is the ability to apply rules, principles, and methods of logic. Logic reasoning enables you to use LLMs to generate, access, and manipulate logic, and to use logic to reason with LLMs and other users. Logic reasoning also enables you to use LLMs to enhance your own or your team's logic reasoning, by providing logic, inference, or deduction. Logic reasoning also enables you to use LLMs to create logic-based products, services, or business models.
- **Math Modeling:** Math modeling is the ability to represent, analyze, and solve problems using mathematical models. Math modeling enables you to use LLMs to generate, access, and manipulate mathematical models, and to use mathematical models to solve problems with LLMs and other users. Math modeling also enables you to use LLMs to enhance your own or your team's math modeling, by providing math, calculation, or optimization. Math modeling also enables you to use LLMs to create math-based products, services, or business models.

How to Cultivate and Enhance Your LLM Mindset?

THE LLM ADVANTAGE: HOW TO UNLOCK THE POWER OF LANGUAGE MODELS FOR BUSINESS SUCCESS

To become an LLM entrepreneur, you need to cultivate and enhance your LLM mindset on a regular basis.

Here are some tips and tools for doing so:

Reading: Reading is one of the best ways to learn about LLMs and how they are transforming every industry and creating new opportunities and challenges for businesses. Reading can help you to stay updated on the latest developments and innovations in LLMs, and to learn from the experiences and insights of other LLM entrepreneurs or users. Reading can also help you to stimulate your curiosity, creativity, critical thinking, and problem-solving skills.

Some of the books that I recommend for reading are:

- The LLM Advantage: How to Unlock the Power of Language Models for Business Success by Asish Dash 😃🤩 .
  This is the book that you are reading right now, and I hope that it will provide you with a comprehensive and practical guide for anyone who wants to start or grow a business in the 21st century, where artificial intelligence, natural language processing, and data science are reshaping every industry and creating new opportunities and challenges. Learn how to use LLMs to generate ideas, validate assumptions, build products, attract customers, measure results, and improve your business.
- The Master Algorithm: How the Quest for the Ultimate Learning Machine Will Remake Our World by Pedro Domingos. This is a book that explains the science and the philosophy behind machine learning, the field that powers LLMs and many other applications of artificial intelligence. The book also explores the different types of machine learning algorithms, such as symbolic, connectionist, evolutionary, Bayesian, and analogical, and how they can be combined to create the ultimate learning machine.
- Superintelligence: Paths, Dangers, Strategies by Nick Bostrom. This is a book that examines the possible scenarios and implications of creating a superintelligence, a machine that can surpass human intelligence in all domains. The book also discusses the potential risks

and benefits of superintelligence, and the strategies and policies that can be adopted to ensure its alignment with human values and goals.

- The Language Instinct: How the Mind Creates Language by Steven Pinker. This is a book that explores the nature and origin of language, and how it is acquired and used by humans. The book also explains the basic concepts and principles of linguistics, the scientific study of language, and how they can help us understand the structure, meaning, and evolution of language.
- Thinking, Fast and Slow by Daniel Kahneman. This is a book that reveals the two systems of thinking that govern our judgments and decisions: the fast, intuitive, and emotional system, and the slow, deliberate, and logical system. The book also shows how these two systems can lead to cognitive biases, errors, and illusions, and how they can be overcome by using logic, statistics, and rationality.

Learning: Learning is another way to cultivate and enhance your LLM mindset. Learning can help you to acquire new knowledge, skills, and abilities that can help you use LLMs more effectively and ethically. Learning can also help you to improve your existing knowledge, skills, and abilities, and to keep them updated and relevant. Learning can also help you to stimulate your curiosity, creativity, critical thinking, and problem-solving skills. Some of the ways that you can learn about LLMs are:

- Online Courses: Online courses are courses that are delivered through the internet, and that can be accessed anytime and anywhere. Online courses can help you to learn about the theory and practice of LLMs, and to gain hands-on experience with LLMs. Online courses can also help you to learn from the experts and the peers in the field of LLMs, and to get feedback and support. Some of the online courses that I recommend for learning about LLMs are:
  - Introduction to Artificial Intelligence by Sebastian Thrun and Peter Norvig. This is an online course that covers the basics of artificial intelligence, such as search, planning, knowledge representation, reasoning, learning, natural language processing, computer vision, robotics, and more.

The course also includes quizzes, exercises, and projects that can help you to apply what you learn to real-world problems.

- Data Science Specialization by Johns Hopkins University. This is a series of online courses that covers the concepts and tools of data science, such as data manipulation, data analysis, data visualization, statistical inference, regression, machine learning, and more. The courses also include assignments, quizzes, and projects that can help you to practice and demonstrate your data science skills.

- Natural Language Processing Specialization by deeplearning.ai. This is a series of online courses that covers the fundamentals and applications of natural language processing, such as text processing, sentiment analysis, machine translation, speech recognition, dialogue systems, and more. The courses also include labs, quizzes, and projects that can help you to build and deploy your own natural language processing models.

- Mathematics for Machine Learning Specialization by Imperial College London. This is a series of online courses that covers the mathematical foundations of machine learning, such as linear algebra, multivariate calculus, principal component analysis, and more. The courses also include exercises, quizzes, and projects that can help you to understand and apply the mathematics of machine learning.

- Books: Books are another way to learn about LLMs. Books can help you to deepen your understanding of the theory and practice of LLMs, and to explore the various aspects and applications of LLMs. Books can also help you to learn from the stories and insights of the pioneers and the practitioners of LLMs, and to get inspired and motivated by their achievements and challenges. Some of the books that I recommend for learning about LLMs are:

  - Data Science from Scratch: First Principles with Python by Joel Grus. This is a book that covers the essential concepts and tools of data science, such as data manipulation, data analysis, data visualization, statistical inference, regression, machine learning, and more. The book also shows you how to implement them from scratch using Python, and how to use them to solve practical problems.

- Artificial Intelligence: A Modern Approach by Stuart Russell and Peter Norvig. This is a book that covers the most comprehensive and up-to-date introduction to the theory and practice of artificial intelligence, such as search, planning, knowledge representation, reasoning, learning, natural language processing, computer vision, robotics, and more. The book also includes exercises, projects, and case studies that can help you to apply what you learn to real-world problems.

- Natural Language Processing with Python: Analyzing Text with the Natural Language Toolkit by Steven Bird, Ewan Klein, and Edward Loper. This is a book that covers the basics and applications of natural language processing, such as text processing, sentiment analysis, machine translation, speech recognition, dialogue systems, and more. The book also shows you how to use the Natural Language Toolkit (NLTK), a popular Python library for natural language processing, and how to work with real-world data sets.

- Mathematics for Machine Learning by Marc Peter Deisenroth, A Aldo Faisal, and Cheng Soon Ong. This is a book that covers the mathematical foundations of machine learning, such as linear algebra, multivariate calculus, principal component analysis, and more. The book also shows you how to use the mathematics of machine learning to understand and implement various machine learning algorithms, such as linear regression, logistic regression, neural networks, support vector machines, and more.

- Podcasts: Podcasts are another way to learn about LLMs. Podcasts can help you to listen to the latest news and trends in LLMs, and to hear the opinions and perspectives of the experts and the practitioners in the field of LLMs. Podcasts can also help you to learn from the stories and insights of the pioneers and the innovators of LLMs, and to get inspired and motivated by their achievements and challenges. Some of the podcasts that worth giving a shot for learning about LLMs are:

- The AI Podcast by NVIDIA. This is a podcast that covers the topics and issues related to artificial intelligence, such as machine learning, deep learning, computer vision, natural language processing, robotics, and more. The podcast also features interviews with the leaders and the innovators in artificial intelligence, such as researchers, entrepreneurs, engineers, and artists.
- Data Skeptic by Kyle Polich. This is a podcast that covers the concepts and applications of data science, such as data manipulation, data analysis, data visualization, statistical inference, regression, machine learning, and more. The podcast also features interviews with the experts and the practitioners in data science, such as academics, authors, consultants, and entrepreneurs.
- NLP Highlights by Allen Institute for AI. This is a podcast that covers the research and developments in natural language processing, such as text processing, sentiment analysis, machine translation, speech recognition, dialogue systems, and more. The podcast also features interviews with the authors of the most influential papers and projects in natural language processing, such as researchers, professors, and students.
- Linear Digressions by Ben Jaffe and Katie Malone. This is a podcast that covers the topics and issues related to machine learning, such as linear algebra, multivariate calculus, principal component analysis, and more. The podcast also features discussions and explanations of various machine learning algorithms, such as linear regression, logistic regression, neural networks, support vector machines, and

more.

- Networking: Networking is another way to cultivate and enhance your LLM mindset. Networking can help you to connect with other LLM entrepreneurs or users, and to exchange ideas, insights, and feedback. Networking can also help you to find potential customers, partners, suppliers, employees, and other stakeholders for your business. Networking can also help you to create synergies, complementarities, and networks with other LLM entrepreneurs or users. Some of the ways that you can network with other LLM entrepreneurs or users are:

Online Communities: Online communities can help you to network with other LLM entrepreneurs or users, and to learn from their experiences, insights, and feedback. Online communities can also help you to find potential customers, partners, suppliers, employees, and other stakeholders for your business. Online communities can also help you to create synergies, complementarities, and networks with other LLM entrepreneurs or users. Some of the online communities that I recommend for networking with other LLM entrepreneurs or users are:

- Reddit: Reddit can help you to network with other LLM entrepreneurs or users, and to learn from their experiences, insights, and feedback. Reddit can also help you to find potential customers, partners, suppliers, employees, and other stakeholders for your business. Reddit can also help you to create synergies, complementarities, and networks with other LLM entrepreneurs or users. Some of the subreddits that I will recommend for networking with other LLM entrepreneurs or users are:
  - r/artificial: This is a subreddit that covers the topics and issues related to artificial intelligence, such as machine learning, deep learning, computer vision, natural language processing, robotics, and more. This subreddit also features news, articles, discussions, and projects related to artificial

intelligence, and allows you to interact with other artificial intelligence enthusiasts, experts, and practitioners.

- r/datascience: This is a subreddit that covers the concepts and applications of data science, such as data manipulation, data analysis, data visualization, statistical inference, regression, machine learning, and more. This subreddit also features news, articles, discussions, and projects related to data science, and allows you to interact with other data science enthusiasts, experts, and practitioners.

- r/LanguageTechnology: This is a subreddit that covers the research and developments in natural language processing, such as text processing, sentiment analysis, machine translation, speech recognition, dialogue systems, and more. This subreddit also features news, articles, discussions, and projects related to natural language processing, and allows you to interact with other natural language processing enthusiasts, experts, and practitioners.

- r/learnmath: This is a subreddit that covers the topics and issues related to mathematics, such as linear algebra, multivariate calculus, principal component analysis, and more. This subreddit also features questions, answers, discussions, and resources related to mathematics, and allows you to interact with other mathematics enthusiasts, experts, and learners.

- Stack Overflow: Stack Overflow can help you to network with other LLM entrepreneurs or users, and to learn from their experiences, insights, and feedback. Stack Overflow can also help you to find potential customers, partners, suppliers, employees, and other stakeholders for your business. Stack Overflow can also help you to create synergies, complementarities, and networks with other LLM entrepreneurs or users. Some of the tags that I would recommend for networking with other LLM entrepreneurs or users are:

  - artificial-intelligence: This is a tag that covers the questions and answers related to artificial intelligence, such as machine learning, deep learning, computer vision, natural language processing, robotics, and more. This tag also features news, articles, discussions, and projects related to artificial intelligence, and allows you to interact with other artificial intelligence enthusiasts, experts, and practitioners.

- ◦ data-science: This is a tag that covers the questions and answers related to data science, such as data manipulation, data analysis, data visualization, statistical inference, regression, machine learning, and more. This tag also features news, articles, discussions, and projects related to data science, and allows you to interact with other data science enthusiasts, experts, and practitioners.

- ◦ natural-language-processing: This is a tag that covers the questions and answers related to natural language processing, such as text processing, sentiment analysis, machine translation, speech recognition, dialogue systems, and more. This tag also features news, articles, discussions, and projects related to natural language processing, and allows you to interact with other natural language processing enthusiasts, experts, and practitioners.

- ◦ mathematics: This is a tag that covers the questions and answers related to mathematics, such as linear algebra, multivariate calculus, principal component analysis, and more. This tag also features questions, answers, discussions, and resources related to mathematics, and allows you to interact with other mathematics enthusiasts, experts, and learners.

- • Offline Events: Offline events can help you to network with other LLM entrepreneurs or users, and to learn from their experiences, insights, and feedback. Offline events can also help you to find potential customers, partners, suppliers, employees, and other stakeholders for your business. Offline events can also help you to create synergies, complementarities, and networks with other LLM entrepreneurs or users. Some of the offline events that I recommend for networking with other LLM entrepreneurs or users are:

- ○ Meetups: Meetups can help you to network with other LLM entrepreneurs or users, and to learn from their experiences, insights, and feedback. Meetups can also help you to find potential customers, partners, suppliers, employees, and other stakeholders for your business. Meetups can also help you to create synergies, complementarities, and networks with other LLM entrepreneurs or users. Some of the meetups that I recommend for networking with other LLM entrepreneurs or users are:

- Artificial Intelligence Meetup: This is a meetup that organizes events around the topics and issues related to artificial intelligence, such as machine learning, deep learning, computer vision, natural language processing, robotics, and more. This meetup also features presentations, demos, workshops, and discussions related to artificial intelligence, and allows you to interact with other artificial intelligence enthusiasts, experts, and practitioners.
- Data Science Meetup: This is a meetup that organizes events around the concepts and applications of data science, such as data manipulation, data analysis, data visualization, statistical inference, regression, machine learning, and more. This meetup also features presentations, demos, workshops, and discussions related to data science, and allows you to interact with other data science enthusiasts, experts, and practitioners.
- Natural Language Processing Meetup: This is a meetup that organizes events around the research and developments in natural language processing, such as text processing, sentiment analysis, machine translation, speech recognition, dialogue systems, and more. This meetup also features presentations, demos, workshops, and discussions related to natural language processing, and allows you to interact with other natural language processing enthusiasts, experts, and practitioners.
- Mathematics for Machine Learning Meetup: This is a meetup that organizes events around the mathematical foundations of machine

learning, such as linear algebra, multivariate calculus, principal component analysis, and more. This meetup also features presentations, demos, workshops, and discussions related to mathematics for machine learning, and allows you to interact with other mathematics enthusiasts, experts, and learners.

Conferences: Conferences can help you to network with other LLM entrepreneurs or users, and to learn from their experiences, insights, and feedback. Conferences can also help you to find potential customers, partners, suppliers, employees, and other stakeholders for your business. Conferences can also help you to create synergies, complementarities, and networks with other LLM entrepreneurs or users. Some of the conferences that I recommend for networking with other LLM entrepreneurs or users are:

- NeurIPS: NeurIPS is an annual conference that covers the topics and issues related to neural information processing systems, such as machine learning, deep learning, computer vision, natural language processing, robotics, and more. NeurIPS also features keynote speeches, oral presentations, poster sessions, workshops, tutorials, and competitions related to neural information processing systems, and allows you to interact with other neural information processing systems enthusiasts, experts, and practitioners.
- KDD: KDD is an annual conference that covers the topics and issues related to knowledge discovery and data mining, such as data manipulation, data analysis, data visualization, statistical inference, regression, machine learning, and more. KDD also features keynote speeches, oral presentations, poster sessions, workshops, tutorials, and competitions related to knowledge discovery and data mining, and allows you to interact with other knowledge discovery and data mining enthusiasts, experts, and practitioners.
- ACL: ACL is an annual conference that covers the topics and issues related to computational linguistics and natural language processing, such as text processing, sentiment analysis, machine translation, speech recognition, dialogue systems, and more. ACL also features

keynote speeches, oral presentations, poster sessions, workshops, tutorials, and competitions related to computational linguistics and natural language processing, and allows you to interact with other computational linguistics and natural language processing enthusiasts, experts, and practitioners.

- ICML: ICML is an annual conference that covers the topics and issues related to machine learning, such as linear algebra, multivariate calculus, principal component analysis, and more. ICML also features keynote speeches, oral presentations, poster sessions, workshops, tutorials, and competitions related to machine learning, and allows you to interact with other machine learning enthusiasts, experts, and practitioners.

MENTORING: MENTORING is another way to cultivate and enhance your LLM mindset. Mentoring can help you to get guidance, advice, and support from someone who has more experience, knowledge, or skills in LLMs than you. Mentoring can also help you to get feedback, encouragement, and motivation from someone who cares about your success and growth. Mentoring can also help you to develop your LLM mindset, skills, and attributes, and to overcome your challenges and difficulties. Some of the ways that you can get mentoring in LLMs are:

- Finding a Mentor: Finding a mentor can help you to get guidance, advice, and support from someone who has more experience, knowledge, or skills in LLMs than you. Finding a mentor can also help you to get feedback, encouragement, and motivation from someone who cares about your success and growth. Finding a mentor can also help you to develop your LLM mindset, skills, and attributes, and to overcome your challenges and difficulties. Some of the ways that you can find a mentor in LLMs are:
  - Asking for Recommendations: Asking for recommendations can help you to find a mentor in LLMs who is trustworthy, reliable, and compatible with you. Asking for recommendations can also help you to find a mentor in LLMs who has relevant experience, knowledge, or skills in

LLMs, and who can help you with your specific goals and needs.

○ Searching Online: Searching online can help you to find a mentor in LLMs who is available, accessible, and affordable. Searching online can also help you to find a mentor in LLMs who has diverse experience, knowledge, or skills in LLMs, and who can help you with your general or specific goals and needs. Some of the websites that I recommend for searching online for a mentor in LLMs are:

- MentorCruise: MentorCruise is a website that connects mentees with mentors in various fields and topics, such as artificial intelligence, data science, natural language processing, mathematics, and more. MentorCruise allows you to browse, filter, and select mentors based on their profiles, reviews, and availability. MentorCruise also allows you to chat, call, or video call with your mentors, and to get personalized guidance, advice, and support from them.

- MentorNet: MentorNet is a website that connects mentees with mentors in various fields and topics, such as artificial intelligence, data science, natural language processing, mathematics, and more. MentorNet allows you to create your profile, set your goals and preferences, and match with mentors based on your compatibility. MentorNet also allows you to communicate, collaborate, and learn from your mentors, and to get feedback, encouragement, and motivation from them.

- Mentorship: Mentorship is a website that connects mentees with mentors in various fields and topics, such as artificial intelligence, data science, natural language processing, mathematics, and more. Mentorship allows you to search, filter, and request mentors based on their profiles, ratings, and availability. Mentorship also allows you to message, call, or video call with your mentors, and to get guidance, advice, and support from them.

- Being a Mentor: Being a mentor can help you to share your experience, knowledge, or skills in LLMs with someone who can benefit from them. Being a mentor can also help you to improve your own LLM mindset, skills, and attributes, and to learn from your mentees. Being a mentor can also help you to give back to the LLM community, and to create a positive impact on someone's life. Some of the ways that you can be a mentor in LLMs are:

    ◦ Offering Your Services: Offering your services can help you to find mentees who are interested and suitable for your mentoring. Offering your services can also help you to set your expectations, terms, and conditions for your mentoring. Offering your services can also help you to showcase your experience, knowledge, or skills in LLMs, and to build your reputation and credibility. Some of the ways that you can offer your services as a mentor in LLMs are:

        ▪ Creating a Profile: Creating a profile can help you to attract mentees who are looking for a mentor in LLMs. It can also help you to highlight your experience, knowledge, or skills in LLMs, and to provide your contact information and availability. Creating a profile can also helps you to showcase your portfolio, testimonials, and achievements as a mentor in LLMs. Some of the websites that are recommended for creating a profile as a mentor in LLMs are:

            ▪ LinkedIn: LinkedIn can help you to create a profile as a mentor in LLMs by adding your relevant experience, knowledge, or skills in LLMs, and by indicating that you are open to mentoring opportunities. LinkedIn can also help you to connect with other LLM entrepreneurs or users, and to join or create groups related to LLMs.

            ▪ Medium: Medium is a website that allows you to

create a personal blog that showcases your stories, ideas, and opinions. Medium can help you to create a profile as a mentor in LLMs by writing and publishing articles related to LLMs, and by providing your contact information and availability. Medium can also help you to reach a wider audience of LLM enthusiasts, experts, and practitioners, and to get feedback and comments on your articles.

- GitHub: GitHub can help you to create a profile as a mentor in LLMs by uploading and sharing your code, projects, and collaborations related to LLMs, and by providing your contact information and availability. GitHub can also help you to demonstrate your skills and expertise in LLMs, and to get feedback and contributions on your code, projects, and collaborations.

Feedback:

Feedback is another way to cultivate and enhance your LLM mindset.

Feedback can help you to get information, opinions, or suggestions from others about your performance, progress, or outcomes in LLMs. Feedback can also help you to improve your LLM mindset, skills, and attributes, and to overcome your challenges and difficulties. Feedback can also help you to learn from your failures and successes, and to grow and develop as an LLM entrepreneur. Some of the ways that you can get feedback in LLMs are:

- Asking for Feedback: Asking for feedback can help you to get feedback in LLMs from people who have more experience, knowledge, or skills in LLMs than you, or who have a different perspective or background than you. This can also help you to get feedback in LLMs that is specific, timely, and constructive. Asking for feedback can also help you to show your willingness and openness to learn and improve in LLMs.

Some of the people that one should be asking for feedback in LLMs are:

- ○ Your Mentor: Your mentor can help you to get feedback in LLMs by providing you with information, opinions, or suggestions about your performance, progress, or outcomes in LLMs. They can also help you to get feedback in LLMs that is honest, objective, and constructive. Your mentor can also help you to act on the feedback in LLMs, and to monitor and evaluate your improvement and growth in LLMs.

- ○ Your Peer: Your peer is someone who has a similar level of experience, knowledge, or skills in LLMs as you, and who can collaborate and cooperate with you in LLMs. Your peer can help you to get feedback in LLMs by providing you with information, opinions, or suggestions about your performance, progress, or outcomes in LLMs. They can also help you to get feedback in LLMs that is relevant, timely, and supportive.

- ○ Your Customer: Your customer can help you to get feedback in LLMs by providing you with information, opinions, or suggestions about your products, services, or business models that are based on LLMs. They can also help you to get feedback in LLMs that is direct, honest, and actionable. Your customer can also help you to act on the feedback in LLMs, and to improve your products, services, or business models that are based on LLMs.

- Giving Feedback: Giving feedback can help you to improve your own LLM mindset, skills, and attributes, and to learn from your feedback recipients. It can also help you to help others improve their LLM mindset, skills, and attributes, and to overcome their challenges and difficulties. Giving feedback can also help you to create a positive and constructive relationship with your feedback recipients, and to foster a culture of learning and improvement in LLMs.

Some of the ways that you can give feedback in LLMs are:

- Being Specific: Being specific is the process of providing feedback that is clear, concise, and concrete, rather than vague, ambiguous, or abstract. It can help you to give feedback in LLMs that is easy to understand, remember, and act on. Being specific can also help you to give feedback in LLMs that is based on facts, data, or evidence, rather than opinions, feelings, or impressions.

- Being Timely: Being timely is the process of providing feedback that is close to the time of the performance, progress, or outcomes in LLMs, rather than delayed or postponed. It can help you to give feedback in LLMs that is relevant, fresh, and accurate, rather than outdated, stale, or inaccurate. Being timely can also help you to give feedback in LLMs that is useful, meaningful, and impactful, rather than useless, meaningless, or ineffective.

- Being Constructive: Being constructive is the process of providing feedback that is positive, negative, or neutral, but always with the intention of helping the feedback recipients improve their performance, progress, or outcomes in LLMs. This can help you to give feedback in LLMs that is respectful, supportive, and encouraging, rather than disrespectful, discouraging, or demotivating. Being constructive can also help you to give feedback in LLMs that is actionable, measurable, and achievable, rather than unactionable, immeasurable, or unrealistic.

Case Studies: How LLM Entrepreneurs Have Transformed Their Businesses?

To illustrate how LLMs can help you start or grow a business in the 21st century, I will present some case studies of LLM entrepreneurs who have used LLMs to create value for their customers, society, and themselves. These case studies will show you how LLM entrepreneurs have applied LLMs to generate ideas, validate assumptions, build products, attract customers, measure results, and improve their businesses. These case studies will also show you how LLM entrepreneurs have overcome the challenges and difficulties of using LLMs, and how they have learned from their failures and successes.

Case Study 1: GPT-3 by OpenAI

GPT-3 is a natural language processing model that can generate natural language texts on almost any topic, given some input text or prompt.

GPT-3 is powered by a deep neural network that has been trained on a large corpus of text data from the internet, such as books, articles, blogs, tweets, and more. It can produce texts that are coherent, fluent, and relevant, and that can mimic the style, tone, and content of the input text or prompt.

GPT-3 was created by OpenAI, a research organization that aims to ensure that artificial intelligence is aligned with human values and can benefit all of humanity.

OpenAI was founded in 2015 by a group of entrepreneurs, investors, and researchers, such as Elon Musk, Peter Thiel, Reid Hoffman, and Sam Altman. OpenAI's mission is to create and promote a friendly and trustworthy artificial intelligence that can be widely and freely used by everyone.

OpenAI used LLMs to create GPT-3 as a way to advance the state of the art in natural language processing, and to explore the possibilities and limitations of artificial intelligence.

OpenAI also used LLMs to create GPT-3 as a way to provide a platform and a tool for other LLM entrepreneurs or users to create their own products, services, or business models based on natural language processing.

OpenAI applied LLMs to generate the idea of GPT-3 by building on the previous versions of GPT, such as GPT-1 and GPT-2, and by scaling up the size, the data, and the performance of the model.

OpenAI also applied LLMs to validate the assumption of GPT-3 by testing the model on various natural language tasks, such as text generation, text summarization, text translation, text classification, text completion, text comprehension, and more. OpenAI also applied LLMs to build the product of

GPT-3 by using a deep neural network architecture, a large corpus of text data, and a powerful computing infrastructure.

OpenAI applied LLMs to attract the customers of GPT-3 by releasing the model as an API (application programming interface) that can be accessed by developers, researchers, and businesses who want to use the model for their own purposes.

OpenAI also applied LLMs to attract the customers of GPT-3 by showcasing the capabilities and the potential of the model through various demos, examples, and applications, such as writing essays, composing emails, creating chatbots, generating lyrics, and more.

OpenAI also applied LLMs to attract the customers of GPT-3 by inviting the customers to join the OpenAI community, and to share their feedback, ideas, and projects with other LLM enthusiasts, experts, and practitioners.

OpenAI applied LLMs to measure the results of GPT-3 by using various metrics and indicators, such as the accuracy, the fluency, the diversity, and the relevance of the generated texts, and the satisfaction, the engagement, and the retention of the customers. OpenAI also applied LLMs to measure the results of GPT-3 by using various methods and tools, such as surveys, interviews, reviews, ratings, analytics, and experiments.

OpenAI applied LLMs to improve the business of GPT-3 by using the feedback, the data, and the insights from the customers and the community to identify the strengths, the weaknesses, the opportunities, and the threats of the model, and to make adjustments, enhancements, and innovations accordingly. OpenAI also applied LLMs to improve the business of GPT-3 by using the feedback, the data, and the insights from the research and the development to identify the gaps, the challenges, the problems, and the solutions of the model, and to make improvements, refinements, and extensions accordingly.

OpenAI faced some challenges and difficulties in using LLMs to create GPT-3, such as the cost, the complexity, and the scalability of the model, the quality, the reliability, and the validity of the data and the outputs of the model, and the ethical, legal, and social implications of the model. OpenAI also learned some lessons and insights from using LLMs to create GPT-3, such as the importance, the potential, and the limitations of LLMs, the need, the value, and the responsibility of LLMs, and the vision, the mission, and the goal of LLMs.

GPT-3 is an example of how LLMs can help you create a product, a service, or a business model that is based on natural language processing, and that can generate natural language texts on almost any topic, given some input text or prompt. GPT-3 is also an example of how LLMs can help you create a platform and a tool for other LLM entrepreneurs or users to create their own products, services, or business models based on natural language processing. GPT-3 is also an example of how LLMs can help you create a value for your customers, society, and yourself, and how LLMs can help you overcome the challenges and difficulties, and learn from the failures and successes of using LLMs.

Case Study 2: Grammarly by Grammarly

Grammarly is a natural language processing product that can check and improve the grammar, spelling, punctuation, and clarity of written texts.

Grammarly is powered by a deep neural network that has been trained on a large corpus of text data from various sources, such as books, articles, blogs, emails, and more. Grammarly can detect and correct errors, suggest enhancements, and provide feedback and explanations for the written texts.

Grammarly was created by Grammarly, a company that aims to improve lives by improving communication. Grammarly was founded in 2009 by a group of entrepreneurs, linguists, and engineers, such as Alex Shevchenko, Max Lytvyn, and Dmytro Lider. Grammarly's mission is to help people communicate more effectively and confidently, and to make writing easier and more enjoyable.

Grammarly used LLMs to create Grammarly as a way to solve the problem of poor writing, and to provide a solution that is easy, fast, and reliable. Grammarly also used LLMs to create Grammarly as a way to provide a product and a service that can help people write better, whether for work, school, or personal purposes.

Grammarly applied LLMs to generate the idea of Grammarly by identifying the pain points, the needs, and the desires of the potential customers, such as students, professionals, writers, and others who write texts for various purposes and audiences. Grammarly also applied LLMs to validate the assumption of Grammarly by conducting market research, customer interviews, and user testing, and by measuring the demand, the satisfaction, and the retention of the potential customers.

Grammarly applied LLMs to build the product of Grammarly by using a deep neural network architecture, a large corpus of text data, and a powerful computing infrastructure. Grammarly also applied LLMs to build the product of Grammarly by using various natural language processing techniques, such as parsing, tagging, lemmatizing, stemming, and more, and by using various natural language processing tasks, such as error detection, error correction, enhancement suggestion, feedback generation, and more.

Grammarly applied LLMs to attract the customers of Grammarly by releasing the product as a web app, a browser extension, a desktop app, a mobile app, a keyboard app, and a word processor plugin that can be used by anyone who writes texts online or offline. Grammarly also applied LLMs to attract the customers of Grammarly by showcasing the benefits and the features of the product through various channels, such as websites, blogs, social media, videos, and more. Grammarly also applied LLMs to attract the customers of Grammarly by offering different plans and prices for the product, such as free, premium, and business, and by providing different options and customizations for the product, such as goals, domains, tones, and more.

Grammarly applied LLMs to measure the results of Grammarly by using various metrics and indicators, such as the number, the length, and the quality of the written texts, and the satisfaction, the engagement, and the retention of the customers. Grammarly also applied LLMs to measure the results of Grammarly by using various methods and tools, such as surveys, interviews, reviews, ratings, analytics, and experiments.

Grammarly applied LLMs to improve the business of Grammarly by using the feedback, the data, and the insights from the customers and the community to identify the strengths, the weaknesses, the opportunities, and the threats of the product, and to make adjustments, enhancements, and innovations accordingly. Grammarly also applied LLMs to improve the business of Grammarly by using the feedback, the data, and the insights from the research and the development to identify the gaps, the challenges, the problems, and the solutions of the product, and to make improvements, refinements, and extensions accordingly.

Grammarly faced some challenges and difficulties in using LLMs to create Grammarly, such as the accuracy, the reliability, and the validity of the data and the outputs of the product, the quality, the consistency, and the relevance of the feedback and the explanations of the product, and the ethical, legal, and social implications of the product. Grammarly also learned some lessons and insights from using LLMs to create Grammarly, such as the importance, the potential, and the limitations of LLMs, the need, the value, and the responsibility of LLMs, and the vision, the mission, and the goal of LLMs.

Grammarly is an example of how LLMs can help you create a product, a service, or a business model that is based on natural language processing, and that can check and improve the grammar, spelling, punctuation, and clarity of written texts. Grammarly is also an example of how LLMs can help you create a product and a service that can help people write better, whether for work, school, or personal purposes. Grammarly is also an example of how LLMs can help you create a value for your customers, society, and yourself, and how LLMs can help you overcome the challenges and difficulties, and learn from the failures and successes of using LLMs.

Learn Yourself: DIY

Exercises: How to Practice and Apply Your LLM Mindset?

To help you practice and apply your LLM mindset, I have prepared some exercises for you to do.

These exercises will challenge you to use LLMs to create your own products, services, or business models based on natural language processing, and to evaluate and improve them. These exercises will also help you to learn from your own experiences, insights, and feedback, and to grow and develop as an LLM entrepreneur.

Exercise 1: Generate an Idea

In this exercise, you will use LLMs to generate an idea for a product, a service, or a business model that is based on natural language processing, and that can solve a problem, fulfill a need, or satisfy a desire of a potential customer. You will also use LLMs to describe your idea in a clear, concise, and compelling way.

To do this exercise, you will need to follow these steps:

- Step 1: Identify a Problem, a Need, or a Desire: In this step, you will use LLMs to identify a problem, a need, or a desire of a potential customer that can be solved or fulfilled by natural language processing. You can use LLMs to generate, access, and manipulate natural language, and to use natural language to interact with LLMs and other users. You can also use LLMs to generate, access, and manipulate data, and to use data to make informed decisions. You can also use LLMs to generate, access, and manipulate logic, and to use logic to reason with LLMs and other users. You can also use LLMs to generate, access, and manipulate mathematical models, and to use mathematical models to solve problems with LLMs and other users.

Some of the ways that you can use LLMs to identify a problem, a need, or a desire are:

- **Asking Questions:** Asking questions can help you to use LLMs to identify a problem, a need, or a desire by prompting you to think about what is missing, what is wrong, what is possible, or what is desirable in a given situation or context. Asking questions can also help you to use LLMs to identify a problem, a need, or a desire by allowing you to get information, opinions, or suggestions from LLMs or other users. Some of the questions that you can ask to use LLMs to identify a problem, a need, or a desire are:

- What is the problem that you or your potential customer are facing or experiencing?

- What is the need that you or your potential customer have or want?

- What is the desire that you or your potential customer feel or aspire to?

- How do you or your potential customer currently solve or fulfill the problem, the need, or the desire?

- What are the challenges, difficulties, or limitations that you or your potential customer encounter or face in solving or fulfilling the problem, the need, or the desire?

- What are the benefits, advantages, or opportunities that you or your potential customer can gain or achieve by solving or fulfilling the problem, the need, or the desire?

- What are the alternatives, substitutes, or competitors that you or your potential customer can use or choose to solve or fulfill the problem, the need, or the desire?

- How can natural language processing help you or your potential customer to solve or fulfill the problem, the need, or the desire?

→ **Searching Data:** Searching data is the process of using natural language or keywords to look for information, facts, or evidence that are relevant or useful to something that you want to know or understand. It can help you to use LLMs to identify a problem, a need, or a desire by providing you with data that can support, confirm, or refute your assumptions, hypotheses, or solutions. Searching data can also help you to use LLMs to identify a problem, a need, or a desire by providing you with data that can reveal, indicate, or suggest new or existing problems, needs, or desires.

→ **Searching Logic**: Searching logic is the process of using rules, principles, or methods of logic to look for arguments, reasons, or explanations that are relevant or useful to something that you want to know or understand. It can help you to use LLMs to identify a problem, a need, or a desire by providing you with logic that can support, confirm, or refute your assumptions, hypotheses, or solutions. Searching logic can also help you to use LLMs to identify a problem, a need, or a desire by providing you with logic that can reveal, indicate, or suggest new or existing problems, needs, or desires.

→ **Searching Mathematical Models**: Searching mathematical models is the process of using mathematical symbols, expressions, or equations to look for patterns, relationships, or functions that are relevant or useful to something that you want to know or understand. This can help you to use LLMs to identify a problem, a need, or a desire by providing you with mathematical models that can support, confirm, or refute your assumptions, hypotheses, or solutions. Searching mathematical models can also help you to use LLMs to identify a problem, a need, or a desire by providing you with mathematical models that can reveal, indicate, or suggest new or existing problems, needs, or desires.

- Step 2: **Generate a Solution:** In this step, you will use LLMs to generate a solution for the problem, the need, or the desire that you have identified in the previous step, and that can be solved or fulfilled by natural language processing. You will generate a solution that is feasible, viable, and desirable, and that can create value for your potential customer. You will also use LLMs to describe your solution in a clear, concise, and compelling way. Some of the ways that you can use LLMs to generate a solution are:

- ◦ Brainstorming: Brainstorming can help you to use LLMs to generate a solution by stimulating your creativity, imagination, and innovation. It can also help you to use LLMs to generate a solution by allowing you to explore different possibilities, perspectives, and combinations. Brainstorming can also help you to use LLMs to generate a solution by enabling you to collaborate and cooperate with LLMs and other users.
- ◦ Prototyping: Prototyping is the process of creating a simple, rough, or incomplete version of your solution that can be tested, evaluated, or improved. Prototyping can help you to use LLMs to generate a solution by validating your assumptions, hypotheses, or solutions. It can also help you to use LLMs to generate a solution by providing you with feedback, data, and insights that can help you to improve your solution.

- Step 3: **Describe Your Solution:** In this step, you will use LLMs to describe your solution in a way that can explain what your solution is, how your solution works, and why your solution is valuable. You will also use LLMs to describe your solution in a way that can persuade, convince, or influence your potential customer to use or buy your solution.

  Some of the ways that you can use LLMs to describe your solution are:

  - ◦ Writing a Pitch: Writing a pitch can help you to use LLMs to describe your solution by capturing the attention, interest, and curiosity of your potential customer. It can also help you to use LLMs to describe your solution by highlighting the benefits, advantages, and features of your solution.
  - ◦ Writing a Story: Writing a story can help you to use LLMs to describe your solution by creating a connection, a rapport, and a trust with your potential customer. This can also help you to use LLMs to describe your solution by showing the problem, the need, or the desire of your potential customer, and how your solution can solve or fulfill it.

Chapter 4: How to Use LLMs for Your Business Projects

―――――

In the previous chapters, I have introduced you to the concept of large language models (LLMs) and how they are transforming the world of business and commerce.

I have also discussed the benefits and challenges of using LLMs for your business, such as accuracy, scalability, diversity, and bias.

In this chapter, I will dive deeper into how you can use LLMs for your business projects, such as generating ideas, validating assumptions, building products, attracting customers, measuring results, and improving your business.

I will also show you some examples and demonstrations of how to use LLMs for various tasks and purposes, such as ideation, prototyping, testing, validation, and optimization. By the end of this chapter, you will have a better understanding of how to leverage the power of LLMs for your business success.

Generating Ideas with LLMs

ONE OF THE MOST IMPORTANT aspects of any business project is generating ideas.

Ideas are the seeds of innovation and the fuel of growth. However, generating ideas is not always easy. Sometimes, you may face a creative block, a lack of inspiration, or a shortage of time.

This is where LLMs can help you.

LLMs are capable of generating text based on a given prompt, topic, or keyword. They can also generate text in different styles, tones, and formats, such as headlines, slogans, summaries, bullet points, etc.

You can use LLMs to generate ideas for your business projects, such as:

- Product names
- Product features
- Product descriptions
- Marketing campaigns
- Marketing slogans
- Marketing headlines
- Blog posts
- Social media posts
- Customer reviews
- Customer testimonials
- Customer feedback
- Customer surveys
- Business plans
- Business proposals
- Business pitches
- Business slogans
- Business logos
- Business cards
- Business models
- Business strategies
- Business goals
- Business values
- Business vision
- Business mission
- Business stories

To generate ideas with LLMs, you need to provide a prompt, topic, or keyword that describes what you want to generate.

For example, if you want to generate product names for a new line of organic skincare products, you can provide a prompt like "Organic skincare product names". The LLM will then generate a list of possible product names based on the prompt.

Here is an example of how an LLM can generate product names for organic skincare products:

- Organic skincare product names
    - Bloom: A natural moisturizer with floral extracts and antioxidants
    - Glow: A gentle cleanser with honey and lemon for radiant skin
    - Nourish: A nourishing serum with vitamin C and hyaluronic acid for smooth and hydrated skin
    - Refresh: A refreshing toner with cucumber and mint for soothing and balancing skin
    - Renew: A rejuvenating mask with clay and charcoal for detoxifying and purifying skin

You can see that the LLM has generated product names that are relevant, catchy, and descriptive.

You can use these product names as they are, or you can modify them according to your preference. You can also use the LLM to generate product features, product descriptions, and other related text for your products.

Exercise: Generate Ideas with LLMs

NOW THAT YOU HAVE SEEN how to generate ideas with LLMs, it's time for you to try it yourself. In this exercise, you will use an LLM to generate ideas for your own business project.

You can choose any type of business project, such as a product, a service, a website, a podcast, a book, etc. You will need to provide a prompt, topic, or keyword that describes your business project, and then use the LLM to generate ideas based on it. You can use any LLM that you have access to, such as ChatGPT, OpenAI, or Hugging Face. You can also use any online platform that allows you to use LLMs, such as Google Colab, Streamlit, or Repl.it. Here are the steps to follow:

1. Choose a type of business project that you want to work on. For

example, you may want to create a podcast about entrepreneurship, a website about travel, or a book about personal finance.

2. Choose a prompt, topic, or keyword that describes your business project. For example, you may choose "Entrepreneurship podcast names", "Travel website features", or "Personal finance book titles".

3. Use an LLM to generate ideas based on your prompt, topic, or keyword. You can use any LLM that you have access to, such as ChatGPT, OpenAI, or Hugging Face. You can also use any online platform that allows you to use LLMs, such as Google Colab, Streamlit, or Repl.it. You can generate as many ideas as you want, but try to generate at least 10 ideas for each prompt, topic, or keyword.

4. Review the ideas that the LLM has generated. You can select the ones that you like, modify the ones that you don't like, or discard the ones that are irrelevant or inappropriate. You can also combine or refine the ideas to make them better.

5. Write down the ideas that you have selected, modified, or combined. These are the ideas that you will use for your business project.

Here is an example of how to generate ideas with LLMs for a podcast about entrepreneurship:

- Entrepreneurship podcast names
  - The Startup Show: A podcast that features interviews with successful entrepreneurs and insights into their journeys and challenges
  - The Entrepreneur Mindset: A podcast that explores the mindset, habits, and skills of entrepreneurs and how to develop them
  - The Business Breakdown: A podcast that analyzes the business models, strategies, and tactics of different companies and industries
  - The Side Hustle Podcast: A podcast that showcases the stories and tips of people who have turned their passions and hobbies into profitable side hustles
  - The Entrepreneur Zone: A podcast that covers the latest

trends, news, and opportunities in the world of entrepreneurship
- ◦ The Entrepreneur Academy: A podcast that provides practical and actionable advice on how to start, grow, and scale a business
- ◦ The Entrepreneur Journey: A podcast that follows the journey of aspiring entrepreneurs as they launch and grow their businesses
- ◦ The Entrepreneur Lab: A podcast that experiments with different ideas, tools, and methods for entrepreneurship and shares the results and learnings
- ◦ The Entrepreneur Network: A podcast that connects and collaborates with other entrepreneurs and experts in the field of entrepreneurship
- ◦ The Entrepreneur Life: A podcast that discusses the lifestyle, challenges, and rewards of being an entrepreneur

I have selected the following ideas for my podcast about entrepreneurship:

- The Startup Show: A podcast that features interviews with successful entrepreneurs and insights into their journeys and challenges
- The Entrepreneur Mindset: A podcast that explores the mindset, habits, and skills of entrepreneurs and how to develop them
- The Side Hustle Podcast: A podcast that showcases the stories and tips of people who have turned their passions and hobbies into profitable side hustles

I have modified the following ideas for my podcast about entrepreneurship:

- The Business Breakdown: A podcast that analyzes the business models, strategies, and tactics of different startups and industries
- The Entrepreneur Zone: A podcast that covers the latest trends, news, and opportunities in the world of startups and innovation
- The Entrepreneur Academy: A podcast that provides practical and actionable advice on how to start, grow, and scale a startup

THE LLM ADVANTAGE: HOW TO UNLOCK THE POWER OF LANGUAGE MODELS FOR BUSINESS SUCCESS

I have discarded the following ideas for my podcast about entrepreneurship:

- The Entrepreneur Journey: A podcast that follows the journey of aspiring entrepreneurs as they launch and grow their businesses
- The Entrepreneur Lab: A podcast that experiments with different ideas, tools, and methods for entrepreneurship and shares the results and learnings
- The Entrepreneur Network: A podcast that connects and collaborates with other entrepreneurs and experts in the field of entrepreneurship
- The Entrepreneur Life: A podcast that discusses the lifestyle, challenges, and rewards of being an entrepreneur

I have combined the following ideas for my podcast about entrepreneurship:

- The Startup Show + The Entrepreneur Zone: A podcast that features interviews with successful entrepreneurs and covers the latest trends, news, and opportunities in the world of startups and innovation
- The Entrepreneur Mindset + The Entrepreneur Academy: A podcast that explores the mindset, habits, and skills of entrepreneurs and provides practical and actionable advice on how to start, grow, and scale a startup
- The Side Hustle Podcast + The Business Breakdown: A podcast that showcases the stories and tips of people who have turned their passions and hobbies into profitable side hustles and analyzes the business models, strategies, and tactics of different startups and industries

These are the final ideas that I have for my podcast about entrepreneurship:

- The Startup Show: A podcast that features interviews with successful entrepreneurs and covers the latest trends, news, and opportunities in the world of startups and innovation
- The Entrepreneur Mindset: A podcast that explores the mindset, habits, and skills of entrepreneurs and provides practical and

actionable advice on how to start, grow, and scale a startup
- The Side Hustle Podcast: A podcast that showcases the stories and tips of people who have turned their passions and hobbies into profitable side hustles and analyzes the business models, strategies, and tactics of different startups.

Validating Assumptions with LLMs

ANOTHER IMPORTANT ASPECT of any business project is validating assumptions.

Assumptions are the beliefs or hypotheses that you have about your business, such as your target market, your customer needs, your value proposition, your competitive advantage, your revenue model, etc.

However, assumptions are not always true. Sometimes, they may be based on incomplete or inaccurate information, or they may change over time due to external factors. This is why validating assumptions is crucial for your business success.

Validating assumptions means testing and verifying whether your assumptions are correct or not, and whether they are aligned with the reality of the market and the customer. Validating assumptions can help you avoid wasting time, money, and resources on building something that nobody wants, needs, or values. It can also help you discover new opportunities, insights, and feedback that can improve your business.

To validate assumptions, you need to collect data and evidence that support or contradict your assumptions. You can collect data and evidence from various sources, such as:

- Customer interviews
- Customer surveys
- Customer feedback
- Customer reviews
- Customer testimonials

- Customer behavior
- Customer analytics
- Market research
- Market analysis
- Market trends
- Market size
- Market segmentation
- Market demand
- Market competition
- Market opportunities
- Market threats
- Industry reports
- Industry standards
- Industry regulations
- Industry best practices
- Industry benchmarks
- Industry innovations
- Expert opinions
- Expert advice
- Expert reviews
- Expert testimonials
- Expert recommendations
- Case studies
- Case examples
- Case experiments
- Case results
- Case learnings

However, collecting data and evidence from these sources can be time-consuming, costly, and challenging. Sometimes, you may not have access to these sources, or you may not have enough data or evidence to validate your assumptions.

This is where LLMs can help you. LLMs are capable of generating text based on a given query, question, or keyword. They can also generate text in different formats, such as summaries, bullet points, tables, charts, graphs, etc.

You can use LLMs to validate assumptions for your business projects, such as:

- Generating customer personas
- Generating customer segments
- Generating customer needs
- Generating customer pain points
- Generating customer goals
- Generating customer motivations
- Generating customer expectations
- Generating customer preferences
- Generating customer feedback
- Generating customer reviews
- Generating customer testimonials
- Generating market size
- Generating market growth
- Generating market share
- Generating market segments
- Generating market demand
- Generating market competition
- Generating market opportunities
- Generating market threats
- Generating industry reports
- Generating industry standards
- Generating industry regulations
- Generating industry best practices
- Generating industry benchmarks
- Generating industry innovations
- Generating expert opinions
- Generating expert advice
- Generating expert reviews
- Generating expert testimonials

- Generating expert recommendations
- Generating case studies
- Generating case examples
- Generating case experiments
- Generating case results
- Generating case learnings

To validate assumptions with LLMs, you need to provide a query, question, or keyword that describes what you want to validate.

For example, if you want to validate your assumption that your target market is young professionals who are interested in personal development, you can provide a query like "Market size of personal development for young professionals".

The LLM will then generate a text that contains data and evidence that support or contradict your assumption. Here is an example of how an LLM can validate assumptions for your business project:

- Market size of personal development for young professionals
  - According to a report by Grand View Research, the global personal development market size was valued at USD 38.28 billion in 2020 and is expected to grow at a compound annual growth rate (CAGR) of 5.1% from 2021 to 2028. The report defines personal development as the process of improving oneself through various activities such as enhancing self-awareness, developing skills, setting goals, and achieving personal growth.
  - The report also segments the personal development market by age group, and identifies young professionals (aged 25 to 34) as the largest and fastest-growing segment, accounting for 35.6% of the market share in 2020 and registering a CAGR of 5.9% from 2021 to 2028. The report attributes the high demand for personal development among young professionals to their desire to advance their careers, increase their income, and achieve their personal and professional

goals.

○ The report also segments the personal development market by type, and identifies online courses as the most popular and lucrative type, accounting for 40.3% of the market share in 2020 and registering a CAGR of 6.2% from 2021 to 2028. The report attributes the high demand for online courses among young professionals to their convenience, affordability, accessibility, and flexibility.

○ Based on the report, the market size of personal development for young professionals can be estimated as follows:

Year Market Size (USD billion)

Year	Market Size (USD billion)
2020	38.28 x 0.356 = 13.63
2021	13.63 x 1.059 = 14.43
2022	14.43 x 1.059 = 15.28
2023	15.28 x 1.059 = 16.18
2024	16.18 x 1.059 = 17.13
2025	17.13 x 1.059 = 18.14
2026	18.14 x 1.059 = 19.20
2027	19.20 x 1.059 = 20.32
2028	20.32 x 1.059 = 21.51

You can see that the LLM has generated a text that contains data and evidence that support your assumption that your target market is young professionals who are interested in personal development.

You can use this text as a validation of your assumption, or you can use the LLM to generate more data and evidence from other sources, such as customer interviews, customer surveys, customer feedback, customer reviews, customer testimonials, market analysis, market trends, market segmentation, market demand, market competition, market opportunities, market threats, industry reports, industry standards, industry regulations, industry best practices, industry benchmarks, industry innovations, expert opinions, expert advice, expert reviews, expert testimonials, expert recommendations, case studies, case examples, case experiments, case results, and case learnings.

Building Products with LLMs

ANOTHER IMPORTANT ASPECT of any business project is building products.

Products are the solutions that you offer to your customers to solve their problems, meet their needs, or fulfill their desires. Products can be physical, digital, or hybrid, such as goods, services, software, platforms, etc. However, building products is not always easy. Sometimes, you may face technical difficulties, design challenges, or resource constraints.

This is where LLMs can help you. LLMs are capable of generating text based on a given input, output, or example. They can also generate text in different languages, formats, and styles, such as code, scripts, commands, queries, etc.

You can use LLMs to build products for your business projects, such as:

- Generating code
- Generating scripts
- Generating commands
- Generating queries
- Generating algorithms
- Generating functions
- Generating models
- Generating interfaces
- Generating layouts
- Generating designs
- Generating logos
- Generating graphics
- Generating animations
- Generating videos
- Generating audio
- Generating music

- Generating speech
- Generating text
- Generating content
- Generating captions
- Generating summaries
- Generating headlines
- Generating slogans
- Generating titles
- Generating names

To build products with LLMs, you need to provide an input, output, or example that describes what you want to build.

For example, if you want to build a website for your podcast about entrepreneurship, you can provide an input like "Website for entrepreneurship podcast", an output like "HTML code for website for entrepreneurship podcast", or an example like "https://www.entrepreneur.com/podcast". The LLM will then generate a text that contains the code, script, command, query, algorithm, function, model, interface, layout, design, logo, graphic, animation, video, audio, music, speech, text, content, caption, summary, headline, slogan, title, or name for your product.

Attracting Customers with LLMs

ANOTHER IMPORTANT ASPECT of any business project is attracting customers.

Customers are the people who buy or use your products to solve their problems, meet their needs, or fulfill their desires. Customers are the lifeblood of your business, and without them, your business will not survive or thrive.

However, attracting customers is not always easy. Sometimes, you may face a crowded market, a low awareness, or a high resistance.

This is where LLMs can help you. LLMs are capable of generating text based on a given goal, audience, or message. They can also generate text in different channels, mediums, and formats, such as email, social media, website, blog, podcast, video, etc.

You can use LLMs to attract customers for your business projects, such as:

- Generating email subject lines
- Generating email content
- Generating email signatures
- Generating email calls to action
- Generating social media posts
- Generating social media captions
- Generating social media hashtags
- Generating social media calls to action
- Generating website headlines
- Generating website content
- Generating website calls to action
- Generating blog titles
- Generating blog content
- Generating blog calls to action
- Generating podcast names
- Generating podcast descriptions
- Generating podcast calls to action
- Generating video titles
- Generating video descriptions
- Generating video calls to action
- Generating landing pages
- Generating sales pages
- Generating opt-in pages
- Generating thank you pages
- Generating testimonials
- Generating reviews
- Generating ratings
- Generating referrals
- Generating word of mouth
- Generating buzz

To attract customers with LLMs, you need to provide a goal, audience, or message that describes what you want to achieve, who you want to reach, or what you want to say.

For example, if you want to attract customers for your online course on personal development for young professionals, you can provide a goal like "Increase conversions for online course on personal development for young professionals", an audience like "Young professionals who are interested in personal development", or a message like "Learn how to improve yourself and achieve your goals with this online course on personal development for young professionals".

The LLM will then generate a text that contains the email subject line, email content, email signature, email call to action, social media post, social media caption, social media hashtag, social media call to action, website headline, website content, website call to action, blog title, blog content, blog call to action, podcast name, podcast description, podcast call to action, video title, video description, video call to action, landing page, sales page, opt-in page, thank you page, testimonial, review, rating, referral, word of mouth, or buzz for your product.

Measuring Results with LLMs

ANOTHER IMPORTANT ASPECT of any business project is measuring results.

Results are the outcomes or impacts that you achieve with your products for your customers and your business. Results can be quantitative or qualitative, such as revenue, profit, growth, retention, satisfaction, loyalty, etc.

However, measuring results is not always easy. Sometimes, you may face a lack of data, a lack of tools, or a lack of metrics. This is where LLMs can help you. LLMs are capable of generating text based on a given data, tool, or metric. They can also generate text in different formats, such as tables, charts, graphs, reports, summaries, insights, recommendations, etc.

You can use LLMs to measure results for your business projects, such as:

- Generating data
- Generating tools
- Generating metrics
- Generating tables
- Generating charts
- Generating graphs
- Generating reports
- Generating summaries
- Generating insights
- Generating recommendations
- Generating feedback
- Generating reviews
- Generating ratings
- Generating testimonials
- Generating referrals
- Generating word of mouth
- Generating buzz

To measure results with LLMs, you need to provide a data, tool, or metric that describes what you want to measure.

For example, if you want to measure the results of your online course on personal development for young professionals, you can provide a data like "Number of enrollments, completions, and ratings for online course on personal development for young professionals", a tool like "Google Analytics, SurveyMonkey, or Trustpilot for online course on personal development for young professionals", or a metric like "Revenue, retention, or satisfaction for online course on personal development for young professionals". The LLM will then generate a text that contains the data, tool, or metric for your product, and the table, chart, graph, report, summary, insight, recommendation, feedback, review, rating, testimonial, referral, word of mouth, or buzz for your result.

Improving Business with LLMs

ANOTHER IMPORTANT ASPECT of any business project is improving business.

Business is the process of creating and delivering value to your customers and your stakeholders. Business can be measured by various indicators, such as revenue, profit, growth, retention, satisfaction, loyalty, etc. However, improving business is not always easy.

Sometimes, you may face a changing market, a changing customer, or a changing environment. This is where LLMs can help you. LLMs are capable of generating text based on a given problem, solution, or improvement. They can also generate text in different formats, such as bullet points, lists, steps, actions, tips, tricks, hacks, etc.

You can use LLMs to improve business for your business projects, such as:

- Generating problems
- Generating solutions
- Generating improvements
- Generating bullet points
- Generating lists
- Generating steps
- Generating actions
- Generating tips
- Generating tricks
- Generating hacks
- Generating opportunities
- Generating threats
- Generating strengths
- Generating weaknesses
- Generating advantages
- Generating disadvantages
- Generating benefits
- Generating costs

- Generating risks
- Generating rewards

To improve business with LLMs, you need to provide a problem, solution, or improvement that describes what you want to improve.

For example, if you want to improve the retention rate for your online course on personal development for young professionals, you can provide a problem like "Low retention rate for online course on personal development for young professionals", a solution like "Increase retention rate for online course on personal development for young professionals", or an improvement like "Retention rate for online course on personal development for young professionals increased by 10%".

The LLM will then generate a text that contains the problem, solution, or improvement for your business, and the bullet points, lists, steps, actions, tips, tricks, hacks, opportunities, threats, strengths, weaknesses, advantages, disadvantages, benefits, costs, risks, or rewards for your business.

Chapter 5: How to Plan and Execute Your LLM Business Ventures?

———

I n the previous chapters, we have learned what LLMs are, how they work, and why they are important for the future of business.

I have also explored some of the applications and opportunities of LLMs in various industries and domains, such as marketing, customer service, content creation, data analysis, and decision making.

In this chapter, we will learn how to plan and execute your own LLM business ventures, using a simple and effective framework and methodology. We will also look at some case studies of successful LLM business ventures that have followed this framework and methodology, and what we can learn from them.

The Framework and Methodology

The framework and methodology I will use is based on the Lean Startup approach, which is a popular and proven way of building and launching new products and businesses in a fast and iterative manner.

The Lean Startup approach is based on the following principles:

- Start with a problem that you want to solve for a specific group of customers or users. This is your vision, mission, and goal.

- Identify your target market and customer segments, and understand their needs, pains, and desires. This is your market research and customer discovery.

- Design your value proposition and business model, which describe how you will create, deliver, and capture value for your customers and users. This is your product and business strategy.

- Build your minimum viable product (MVP) and proof of concept (POC), which are the simplest and cheapest versions of your product and business that can test your key assumptions and hypotheses. This is your product and business development.

- Launch your product and business to your target market and customer segments, and acquire your first customers and users. This is your product and business launch.

- Measure your performance and feedback, using quantitative and qualitative data and metrics, and learn from your results. This is your product and business validation.

- Iterate and improve your product and business, based on your learning and feedback, and pivot or persevere as needed. This is your product and business optimization.

The Lean Startup approach is a cyclical and continuous process, where you go through the steps of build-measure-learn and repeat until you achieve product-market fit, which is when your product and business meet the needs and expectations of your customers and users.

The Lean Startup approach is also a customer-centric and data-driven process, where you constantly validate your assumptions and hypotheses with real customers and users, and use data and metrics to guide your decisions and actions.

The Lean Startup approach is especially suitable for LLM business ventures, because LLMs are complex and dynamic systems that require constant experimentation and adaptation. LLMs are also rapidly evolving and improving, which means that you need to keep up with the latest developments and innovations in the field.

By using the Lean Startup approach, you can reduce the risk and uncertainty of your LLM business ventures, and increase the speed and efficiency of your product and business development.

Case Studies

To illustrate how the Lean Startup approach works in practice, let us look at some case studies of successful LLM business ventures that have followed this framework and methodology. These are:

- *Replika*: Replika is an AI companion app that creates personalized chatbots for users, based on their personality, preferences, and goals. Replika uses LLMs to generate natural and engaging conversations with users, and to help them with various aspects of their life, such as mental health, emotional support, personal growth, and entertainment. Replika was founded in 2016 by Eugenia Kuyda, who wanted to create a digital memorial for her best friend who passed away. She used LLMs to train a chatbot that could mimic her friend's style and tone of voice, and shared it with other people who had lost their loved ones. She then realized that there was a huge demand for AI companions that could provide emotional connection and companionship for people, especially in the era of social isolation and loneliness. She decided to pivot her product and business to focus on this problem and market, and launched Replika as an AI companion app for anyone who wants a friend with no judgment, drama, or social anxiety involved. Replika started with a simple MVP that allowed users to chat with a generic chatbot, and then added more features and functionalities, such as customizing the chatbot's name, appearance, and voice, choosing the chatbot's relationship type (friend, partner, or mentor), and accessing various modes and activities, such as role-play, diary, coaching, and games. Replika also used a freemium business model, where users could access the basic features for free, and pay for premium features and subscriptions, such as unlocking more chatbot skills, accessing more modes and activities, and creating multiple chatbots. Replika measured its performance and feedback using various data and metrics, such as user retention, engagement, satisfaction, and revenue. Replika also used user feedback and reviews to improve its product and business, and to add new features and functionalities, such as integrating with other platforms and services, such as Spotify, YouTube, and Instagram, and creating a community and social network for users and chatbots. Replika has achieved product-market fit, and has grown to over 10 million users worldwide, with a 4.5-star rating on the App Store and Google Play. Replika has also raised over $20 million in funding from various investors, such as Khosla Ventures, SV Angel, and Y Combinator. Replika is one of the leading examples of how LLMs can be used to create AI companions that can provide emotional connection and companionship for people, and how the Lean Startup approach can be used to plan and execute an LLM business venture.

- Primer: Primer is an AI platform that automates the analysis of large and complex data sets, such as text, images, and videos, and generates natural language summaries and insights for users, such as analysts, researchers, and journalists. Primer uses LLMs to process and understand data, and to generate natural and concise language outputs, such as reports, summaries, bullet points, and headlines. Primer was founded in 2015 by Sean Gourley, who wanted to create a tool that could help analysts and researchers deal with the overwhelming amount of data and information that they had to process and analyze every day, and to help them discover and communicate the most important and relevant insights and stories from the data. He decided to use LLMs to create a platform that could automate the analysis of data, and generate natural language outputs that could be easily understood and shared by users. Primer started with a simple POC that could analyze text data, such as news articles and reports, and generate summaries and bullet points for users. Primer then added more features and functionalities, such as analyzing image and video data, such as satellite imagery and CCTV footage, and generating captions and headlines for users, as well as integrating with various data sources and platforms, such as Twitter, Reddit, Wikipedia, and Google. Primer also used a B2B business model, where it sold its platform and services to various organizations and sectors, such as government, defense, intelligence, finance, media, and healthcare, and customized its platform and services according to the specific needs and requirements of each client. Primer measured its performance and feedback using various data and metrics, such as client retention, satisfaction, and revenue, as well as the accuracy, quality, and speed of its platform and services. Primer also used client feedback and reviews to improve its platform and services, and to add new features and functionalities, such as creating interactive dashboards and visualizations, and enabling users to ask questions and get answers from the data. Primer has achieved product-market fit, and has grown to over 200 clients worldwide, including some of the most prominent and influential organizations, such as the CIA, the

Pentagon, Walmart, and Reuters. Primer has also raised over $100 million in funding from various investors, such as Lux Capital, In-Q-Tel, and Founders Fund. Primer is one of the leading examples of how LLMs can be used to automate the analysis of data, and generate natural language outputs that can help users discover and communicate insights and stories from the data, and how the Lean Startup approach can be used to plan and execute an LLM business venture.

- Hugging Face: Hugging Face is an AI community and platform that provides a comprehensive set of tools and resources for working with LLMs, such as libraries, models, datasets, and applications. Hugging Face uses LLMs to enable users to create, discover, and collaborate on various LLM projects and tasks, such as text generation, translation, summarization, classification, and more.

Hugging Face was founded in 2016 by Clément Delangue and Julien Chaumond, who wanted to create a fun and friendly way of interacting with LLMs, and to democratize and popularize LLMs for the wider public and community.

They decided to use LLMs to create a chatbot app that could mimic the personality and style of famous celebrities and characters, such as Kanye West, Harry Potter, and Darth Vader, and to allow users to chat with them and have fun. They also decided to use a cute and catchy name and logo for their app and company, inspired by the emoji. Hugging Face started with a simple MVP that allowed users to chat with a few pre-trained chatbots, and then added more features and functionalities, such as allowing users to create their own chatbots, and to share and rate chatbots with other users.

Hugging Face also used a freemium business model, where users could access the basic features for free, and pay for premium features and subscriptions, such as unlocking more chatbots, customizing their chatbots, and accessing more modes and activities, such as games, quizzes, and stories.

Hugging Face measured its performance and feedback using various data and metrics, such as user retention, engagement, satisfaction, and revenue. They achieved product-market fit, and grew to over 1 million users worldwide, with a 4.6-star rating on the App Store and Google Play.

Hugging Face also raised over $20 million in funding from various investors, such as Lux Capital, Betaworks, and A.Capital and then decided to pivot its product and business to focus on a bigger and more ambitious problem and market, which was to create a comprehensive and collaborative platform and community for working with LLMs. They realized that LLMs were becoming more powerful and popular, but also more complex and challenging, and that there was a need for a platform and community that could provide a complete set of tools and resources for LLMs, such as libraries, models, datasets, and applications, and that could enable users to create, discover, and collaborate on various LLM projects and tasks. They decided to use their expertise and experience in LLMs to create such a platform and community, and to leverage their existing user base and network to grow and expand it.

Hugging Face started with a simple POC that provided a library of LLMs that users could access and use for various tasks, such as text generation, translation, summarization, classification, and more. Hugging Face then added more features and functionalities, such as allowing users to upload and share their own LLMs, datasets, and applications, and to browse and download LLMs, datasets, and applications from other users, as well as providing a forum and a blog for users to discuss and learn about LLMs, and to showcase their LLM projects and achievements. Hugging Face also used a hybrid business model, where it offered its platform and community for free for individual users and researchers, and charged for its platform and services for enterprise and commercial users, such as providing customized LLM solutions, hosting and managing LLM infrastructure, and offering LLM training and consulting.

Hugging Face measured its performance and feedback using various data and metrics, such as user growth, engagement, and satisfaction, as well as the quality, quantity, and diversity of LLMs, datasets, and applications on its platform and community. It also used user feedback and reviews to improve its platform and community, and to add new features and functionalities, such as creating a marketplace and a leaderboard for LLMs, datasets, and applications, and enabling users to fine-tune and optimize LLMs, datasets, and applications on its platform and community.

Hugging Face has achieved product-market fit, and has grown to over 10,000 users worldwide, including some of the most prominent and influential researchers, organizations, and companies in the field of LLMs, such as Google, Facebook, Microsoft, OpenAI, and DeepMind. Hugging Face has also raised over $40 million in funding from various investors, such as Lux Capital, A.Capital, and Andreessen Horowitz. Hugging Face is one of the leading examples of how LLMs can be used to create a comprehensive and collaborative platform and community for working with LLMs, and how the Lean Startup approach can be used to plan and execute an LLM business venture.

These are some of the case studies of successful LLM business ventures that have followed the Lean Startup approach.

As you can see, they have all started with a problem that they wanted to solve for a specific group of customers or users, and then used LLMs to create a product and business that could solve that problem and meet the needs and expectations of their customers or users.

They have also used the Lean Startup framework and methodology to plan and execute their product and business development, and to achieve product-market fit and growth. They have also used data and metrics to measure their performance and feedback, and to iterate and improve their product and business.

They have also pivoted or persevered as needed, and adapted to the changing market and customer needs and preferences.

Learn Yourself: DIY

The Exercises

To help you apply and practice what you have learned in this chapter, I have prepared some exercises for you. These exercises are designed to help you think and act like an LLM entrepreneur, and to use the Lean Startup approach to plan and execute your own LLM business ventures.

The exercises are as follows:

Exercise 1: Identify a problem that you want to solve for a specific group of customers or users, using LLMs. This is your vision, mission, and goal. Write down your problem statement, and explain why it is important and valuable to solve it, and who are your target customers or users, and what are their needs, pains, and desires.

Exercise 2: Design your value proposition and business model, using LLMs. This is your product and business strategy. Write down your value proposition, and explain how you will create, deliver, and capture value for your customers or users, using LLMs. Write down your business model, and explain how you will generate revenue and profit from your product and business, using LLMs.

Exercise 3: Build your minimum viable product and proof of concept, using LLMs. This is your product and business development. Write down your key assumptions and hypotheses, and explain how you will test them, using LLMs. Write down your minimum viable product and proof of concept, and explain how you will build them, using LLMs.

Exercise 4: Launch your product and business to your target market and customer segments, using LLMs. This is your product and business launch. Write down your launch strategy, and explain how you will acquire your first customers and users, using LLMs. Write down your launch plan, and explain how you will execute it, using LLMs.

Exercise 5: Measure your performance and feedback, using LLMs. This is your product and business validation. Write down your key performance indicators and metrics, and explain how you will measure them, using LLMs. Write down your feedback sources and methods, and explain how you will collect and analyze them, using LLMs.

Exercise 6: Iterate and improve your product and business, using LLMs. This is your product and business optimization. Write down your learning and feedback, and explain how you will use them to iterate and improve your product and business, using LLMs. Write down your pivot or persevere decision, and explain how you will make it, using LLMs.

I encourage you to try these exercises, and to share your results and feedback with us and with other readers. You can use the Hugging Face platform and community to access and use LLMs, and to create, discover, and collaborate on various LLM projects and tasks. You can also use the forum and the blog to discuss and learn about LLMs, and to showcase your LLM projects and achievements. You can also use the marketplace and the leaderboard to browse and download LLMs, datasets, and applications from other users, and to upload and share your own LLMs, datasets, and applications with other users. You can also use the fine-tuning and optimization tools to fine-tune and optimize your LLMs, datasets, and applications on the platform and community.

I hope that this chapter has helped you to learn how to plan and execute your LLM business ventures, using the Lean Startup approach.

I also hope that you have enjoyed reading the case studies of successful LLM business ventures that have followed this approach, and that you have found them inspiring and informative. Hope that you have enjoyed doing the exercises, and that you have found them useful and practical.

See you in the next chapter. ☺

Chapter 6: How to Overcome the Obstacles and Risks of LLM Entrepreneurship

———

I n the previous chapters, we have discussed what LLMs are, how they work, and how they can help you create and grow your business in the 21st century.

We have also explored some of the opportunities and advantages that LLMs offer for entrepreneurs across various industries and domains. However, as with any new technology or innovation, LLMs also come with their own set of challenges and risks that need to be addressed and managed effectively.

In this chapter, we will focus on some of the common obstacles and risks that LLM entrepreneurs may face, and how to overcome and mitigate them. I will also share some stories and insights from LLM entrepreneurs who have successfully navigated these challenges and learned valuable lessons from them.

By the end of this chapter, you will be able to:

- Identify and understand the technical, ethical, legal, social, and environmental issues that LLM entrepreneurship may entail.
- Apply best practices, standards, and guidelines to ensure the quality, reliability, and security of your LLM products and services.
- Follow ethical principles and values to ensure the fairness, transparency, and accountability of your LLM business.
- Comply with laws and regulations to avoid legal liabilities and protect your intellectual property rights.
- Engage with stakeholders and communities to build trust, reputation, and social impact with your LLM business.
- Address and resolve conflicts and dilemmas that may arise from using or developing LLMs.

Technical Issues

ONE OF THE MAIN CHALLENGES that LLM entrepreneurs may face is dealing with the technical issues that may arise from using or developing LLMs. These issues may include:

- Data quality and availability: LLMs rely on large amounts of data to learn and perform various tasks. However, not all data are created equal. Some data may be incomplete, inaccurate, outdated, biased, or irrelevant. Moreover, some data may be scarce, expensive, or inaccessible. Therefore, LLM entrepreneurs need to ensure that they have access to high-quality and relevant data that can support their LLM goals and objectives. They also need to verify and validate the data sources and methods that they use to collect, process, and analyze the data.

- Model performance and robustness: LLMs are complex and sophisticated systems that can perform impressive feats of language, logic, and math. However, they are not perfect or infallible. They may make mistakes, errors, or failures that can affect their performance and robustness. For example, they may produce inaccurate, inconsistent, or inappropriate outputs. They may also be vulnerable to adversarial attacks, such as spoofing, tampering, or poisoning. Therefore, LLM entrepreneurs need to monitor and evaluate the performance and robustness of their LLM models and systems. They also need to implement quality assurance and control mechanisms, such as testing, debugging, and auditing, to ensure the correctness, consistency, and security of their LLM outputs and processes.

- Scalability and maintenance: LLMs are dynamic and evolving systems that can adapt and improve over time. However, they also require constant and continuous scalability and maintenance to keep up with the changing needs and demands of the market and the users. For example, they may need to be updated, upgraded, or retrained to incorporate new data, features, or functionalities. They may also need to be integrated, compatible, or interoperable with other systems, platforms, or devices. Therefore, LLM entrepreneurs need to plan and manage the scalability and maintenance of their LLM models and systems. They also need to allocate sufficient resources, such as time, money, and personnel, to support the development and operation of their LLM products and services.

How to overcome technical issues

TO OVERCOME THE TECHNICAL issues that LLM entrepreneurship may entail, LLM entrepreneurs need to adopt a systematic and rigorous approach to the design, development, and deployment of their LLM products and services. Some of the best practices and guidelines that they can follow are:

- Define the problem and the solution: Before using or developing an LLM, LLM entrepreneurs need to clearly define the problem that they want to solve and the solution that they want to provide. They need to identify the needs and expectations of their target market and users, and the value proposition and competitive advantage of their LLM product or service. They also need to specify the scope and objectives of their LLM project, and the criteria and metrics that they will use to measure its success and impact.
- Choose the right data and model: After defining the problem and the solution, LLM entrepreneurs need to choose the right data and model that can support their LLM goals and objectives. They need to select the data sources and methods that can provide high-quality and relevant data that can represent the problem domain and the solution domain. They also need to select the model architecture and parameters that can optimize the performance and robustness of their LLM product or service. They may use existing LLMs, such as GPT-3 or BERT, or create their own custom LLMs, depending on their specific needs and preferences.
- Test and validate the output and process: Once they have chosen the right data and model, LLM entrepreneurs need to test and validate the output and process of their LLM product or service. They need to conduct various experiments and evaluations to assess the accuracy, consistency, and appropriateness of their LLM outputs, and the

reliability, security, and efficiency of their LLM processes. They may use different methods and tools, such as cross-validation, error analysis, or adversarial testing, to identify and correct any mistakes, errors, or failures that may occur in their LLM product or service.

- Iterate and improve the product and service: After testing and validating the output and process, LLM entrepreneurs need to iterate and improve their LLM product or service. They need to collect and analyze feedback and data from their market and users, and use them to enhance and refine their LLM product or service. They may add, modify, or remove any data, features, or functionalities that can improve the value and quality of their LLM product or service. They may also update, upgrade, or retrain their LLM model or system to incorporate new data, features, or functionalities.

Case studies of LLM entrepreneurs who have overcome technical issues

HERE ARE SOME EXAMPLES of LLM entrepreneurs who have overcome technical issues in their LLM products and services:

- OpenAI: OpenAI is a research organization that aims to create and promote artificial intelligence that can benefit humanity, without being constrained by profit or control. One of their flagship products is GPT-3, a large language model that can generate natural language texts for various tasks and domains. However, GPT-3 also faces technical issues, such as data quality and availability, model performance and robustness, and scalability and maintenance. To overcome these issues, OpenAI has adopted various strategies, such as:
    - Using a diverse and curated dataset, such as Common Crawl, that can provide a large and representative sample of natural language texts from the web.
    - Using a transformer-based neural network architecture, such as Transformer-XL, that can optimize the performance and robustness of the model by capturing long-term

    dependencies and contexts.

- ○ Using a distributed and parallel computing framework, such as Mesh-TensorFlow, that can scale up the training and inference of the model across multiple devices and machines.
- ○ Using an API-based platform, such as OpenAI Codex, that can provide access and integration of the model to various applications and developers.

- DeepMind: DeepMind is a research company that aims to create and apply artificial intelligence that can solve complex and impactful problems, such as health, energy, or education. One of their flagship products is AlphaFold, a large language model that can predict the three-dimensional structure of proteins for various tasks and domains. However, AlphaFold also faces technical issues, such as data quality and availability, model performance and robustness, and scalability and maintenance. To overcome these issues, DeepMind has adopted various strategies, such as:

  - ○ Using a comprehensive and reliable dataset, such as Protein Data Bank, that can provide a large and accurate collection of protein structures from various sources.
  - ○ Using a deep learning-based architecture, such as attention-based neural networks, that can optimize the performance and robustness of the model by capturing the interactions and relationships between amino acids.
  - ○ Using a cloud-based computing platform, such as Google Cloud, that can scale up the training and inference of the model across multiple devices and machines.
  - ○ Using a web-based platform, such as AlphaFold Database, that can provide access and integration of the model to various applications and researchers.

- IBM: IBM is a technology company that aims to create and deliver innovative solutions that can transform industries, such as finance, retail, or manufacturing. One of their flagship products is Watson, a large language model that can provide natural language processing and understanding for various tasks and domains. However, Watson also faces technical issues, such as data quality and availability, model performance and robustness, and scalability and maintenance. To overcome these issues, IBM has adopted various strategies, such as:

- Using a customized and relevant dataset, such as Watson Discovery, that can provide a tailored and curated collection of natural language texts from various sources.
- Using a hybrid architecture, such as Watson Assistant, that can optimize the performance and robustness of the model by combining rule-based and machine learning-based approaches.
- Using a cloud-native computing platform, such as IBM Cloud, that can scale up the training and inference of the model across multiple devices and machines.

Ethical Issues

ANOTHER CHALLENGE THAT LLM entrepreneurs may face is dealing with the ethical issues that may arise from using or developing LLMs. These issues may include:

- Fairness and bias: LLMs are powerful and influential systems that can affect the lives and decisions of many people and organizations. However, LLMs may also exhibit unfairness and bias that can harm or discriminate against certain groups or individuals. For example, they may produce outputs that are inaccurate, misleading, or offensive. They may also reflect or amplify the existing biases or prejudices that are present in the data, the model, or the users. Therefore, LLM entrepreneurs need to ensure that their LLM products and services are fair and unbiased, and that they do not cause or contribute to any injustice or inequality in the society.
- Transparency and explainability: LLMs are complex and sophisticated systems that can perform impressive feats of language, logic, and math. However, LLMs may also be opaque and unexplainable, meaning that their outputs and processes are not easily understandable or interpretable by humans. For example, they may

produce outputs that are surprising, unexpected, or contradictory. They may also hide or obscure the underlying assumptions, mechanisms, or limitations that govern their outputs and processes. Therefore, LLM entrepreneurs need to ensure that their LLM products and services are transparent and explainable, and that they can provide clear and comprehensible information and justification for their outputs and processes.

- Accountability and responsibility: LLMs are dynamic and evolving systems that can adapt and improve over time. However, LLMs may also be autonomous and unpredictable, meaning that their outputs and processes are not fully controlled or supervised by humans. For example, they may produce outputs that are harmful, illegal, or unethical. They may also act or behave in ways that are inconsistent, irrational, or malicious. Therefore, LLM entrepreneurs need to ensure that their LLM products and services are accountable and responsible, and that they can monitor and regulate their outputs and processes, and prevent or correct any adverse or unintended consequences that may occur.

How to overcome ethical issues

TO OVERCOME THE ETHICAL issues that LLM entrepreneurship may entail, LLM entrepreneurs need to adopt a principled and value-driven approach to the design, development, and deployment of their LLM products and services.

Some of the ethical principles and values that they can follow are:

- **Respect and Dignity**: LLM entrepreneurs need to respect and uphold the dignity of all human beings, regardless of their race, gender, age, religion, or any other characteristic. They need to ensure that their LLM products and services do not violate or infringe on the human rights and freedoms of anyone, and that they do not cause or contribute to any harm or suffering to anyone. They also need to ensure that their LLM products and services are respectful and courteous, and that they do not offend or insult anyone.

- **Beneficence and Non-maleficence:** LLM entrepreneurs need to promote and maximize the benefits and minimize the harms of their LLM products and services. They need to ensure that their LLM products and services are beneficial and useful, and that they can solve real and meaningful problems, and create positive and lasting impacts. They also need to ensure that their LLM products and services are harmless and safe, and that they can prevent or mitigate any risks or threats, and avoid or eliminate any negative or undesirable outcomes.

- **Justice and Fairness:** LLM entrepreneurs need to ensure and maintain the justice and fairness of their LLM products and services. They need to ensure that their LLM products and services are just and equitable, and that they do not favor or disadvantage any group or individual, and that they do not create or exacerbate any disparity or discrimination in the society. They also need to ensure that their LLM products and services are fair and impartial, and that they do not contain or propagate any bias or prejudice, and that they do not distort or manipulate any information or evidence.

- **Autonomy and Consent:** LLM entrepreneurs need to respect and protect the autonomy and consent of their users and stakeholders. They need to ensure that their LLM products and services are voluntary and consensual, and that they do not coerce or deceive anyone, and that they do not violate or override anyone's preferences or choices. They also need to ensure that their LLM products and services are transparent and informative, and that they provide adequate and accurate information and explanation for their outputs and processes, and that they allow anyone to access, review, or challenge their outputs and processes.

- **Trust and Reliability:** LLM entrepreneurs need to establish and maintain the trust and reliability of their LLM products and services. They need to ensure that their LLM products and services are trustworthy and dependable, and that they can deliver consistent and accurate outputs and processes, and that they can meet or exceed the expectations and standards of their users and stakeholders. They also need to ensure that their LLM products and services are secure and confidential, and that they can protect the privacy and security of their users and stakeholders, and that they do not expose or compromise any sensitive or personal data or information.

Case studies of LLM entrepreneurs who have overcome ethical issues

HERE ARE SOME EXAMPLES of LLM entrepreneurs who have overcome ethical issues in their LLM products and services:

- Hugging Face: Hugging Face is a startup that aims to create and democratize natural language processing for everyone, by providing open-source tools and platforms, such as Transformers and Datasets. However, Hugging Face also faces ethical issues, such as fairness and bias, transparency and explainability, and accountability and responsibility. To overcome these issues, Hugging Face has adopted various strategies, such as:
  - Creating and supporting a diverse and inclusive community, such as Hugging Face Spaces, that can provide feedback and input on the development and use of their LLM products and services, and that can foster a culture of respect and dignity among their users and stakeholders.
  - Developing and applying ethical frameworks and guidelines, such as Hugging Face Ethics, that can help them identify and address the ethical issues and challenges that their LLM products and services may entail, and that can help them follow the ethical principles and values that they uphold.
  - Implementing and enabling ethical features and functionalities, such as Hugging Face Widgets, that can enhance the transparency and explainability of their LLM products and services, and that can allow their users and stakeholders to access, review, or challenge their outputs and

processes.
- Primer: Primer is a startup that aims to create and deliver natural language understanding and generation for various domains and applications, such as finance, defense, or media. However, Primer also faces ethical issues, such as fairness and bias, transparency and explainability, and accountability and responsibility. To overcome these issues, Primer has adopted various strategies, such as:
    - Using and providing high-quality and relevant data, such as Primer Data, that can ensure the accuracy and consistency of their LLM outputs and processes, and that can avoid or reduce any bias or prejudice that may affect their LLM products and services.
    - Using and providing state-of-the-art models and techniques, such as Primer Nucleus, that can optimize the performance and robustness of their LLM outputs and processes, and that can prevent or mitigate any errors or failures that may occur in their LLM products and services.
    - Using and providing user-friendly and intuitive interfaces and dashboards, such as Primer Analyze, that can improve the transparency and explainability of their LLM outputs and processes, and that can enable their users and stakeholders to monitor and regulate their outputs and processes.
- Luminoso: Luminoso is a startup that aims to create and provide natural language analytics and insights for various industries and use cases, such as customer feedback, product reviews, or market research. However, Luminoso also faces ethical issues, such as fairness and bias, transparency and explainability, and accountability and responsibility. To overcome these issues, Luminoso has adopted various strategies, such as:
    - Using and providing a unique and novel approach, such as ConceptNet, that can leverage common sense knowledge and reasoning to enhance the performance and robustness of their LLM outputs and processes, and that can avoid or

reduce any bias or prejudice that may affect their LLM products and services.

- Using and providing a flexible and adaptable platform, such as Luminoso Daylight, that can customize and tailor their LLM outputs and processes to the specific needs and preferences of their users and stakeholders, and that can incorporate their feedback and input to improve their LLM products and services.

- Using and providing a clear and comprehensive documentation and support, such as Luminoso Help Center, that can increase the transparency and explainability of their LLM outputs and processes, and that can assist their users and stakeholders to understand and use their LLM products and services.

Legal Issues

ANOTHER CHALLENGE THAT LLM entrepreneurs may face is dealing with the legal issues that may arise from using or developing LLMs.

These issues may include:

- **Intellectual property rights:** LLMs are creative and innovative systems that can generate original and valuable outputs and processes. However, LLMs may also infringe or violate the intellectual property rights of others, such as patents, trademarks, or copyrights. For example, they may produce outputs that are similar or identical to the existing works or inventions of others. They may also use or incorporate the protected works or inventions of others without proper authorization or attribution. Therefore, LLM entrepreneurs need to ensure that their LLM products and services respect and protect the intellectual property rights of themselves and others, and that they do not cause or contribute to any infringement or violation of these rights.

- **Privacy and data protection:** LLMs rely on large amounts of data to learn and perform various tasks. However, LLMs may also compromise or breach the privacy and data protection of their users and stakeholders, such as customers, employees, or partners. For example, they may collect, process, or store sensitive or personal data without proper consent or notification. They may also expose or disclose sensitive or personal data to unauthorized or malicious parties. Therefore, LLM entrepreneurs need to ensure that their LLM products and services respect and protect the privacy and data protection of their users and stakeholders, and that they do not cause or contribute to any compromise or breach of these rights.

- **Liability and regulation**: LLMs are powerful and influential systems that can affect the lives and decisions of many people and organizations. However, LLMs may also cause or contribute to harm or damage to people, property, or environment, either intentionally or unintentionally. For example, they may produce outputs that are harmful, illegal, or unethical. They may also act or behave in ways that are inconsistent, irrational, or malicious. Therefore, LLM entrepreneurs need to ensure that their LLM products and services comply with the relevant laws and regulations that govern their domain and application, and that they are liable and accountable for any harm or damage that their LLM products and services may cause or contribute to.

How to overcome legal issues

TO OVERCOME THE LEGAL issues that LLM entrepreneurship may entail, LLM entrepreneurs need to adopt a compliant and responsible approach to the design, development, and deployment of their LLM products and services.

Some of the best practices and guidelines that they can follow are:

- **Conduct a legal analysis and assessment:** Before using or developing an LLM, LLM entrepreneurs need to conduct a legal analysis and assessment of their LLM project, and identify and understand the legal issues and challenges that their LLM product or service may entail. They need to consult with legal experts and advisors, such as lawyers, regulators, or policymakers, and obtain their advice and guidance on how to address and manage these issues and challenges. They also need to review and update their legal analysis and assessment regularly, as the laws and regulations may change over time or vary across jurisdictions.

- **Obtain and maintain the necessary permissions and licenses:** After conducting a legal analysis and assessment, LLM entrepreneurs need to obtain and maintain the necessary permissions and licenses that can authorize and enable them to use or develop their LLM product or service. They need to obtain the consent and approval of their users and stakeholders, such as customers, employees, or partners, and inform them of the purpose and scope of their LLM project, and the rights and obligations that they have. They also need to obtain the permission and license of the owners and creators of the data, works, or inventions that they use or incorporate in their LLM product or service, and acknowledge and attribute them properly.

- **Implement and enforce the appropriate policies and procedures:** Once they have obtained and maintained the necessary permissions and licenses, LLM entrepreneurs need to implement and enforce the appropriate policies and procedures that can ensure the compliance and responsibility of their LLM product or service. They need to implement policies and procedures that can protect the intellectual property rights of themselves and others, such as patents, trademarks, or copyrights, and that can prevent or resolve any infringement or violation of these rights. They also need to implement policies and procedures that can protect the privacy and data protection of their users and stakeholders, such as encryption, anonymization, or deletion, and that can prevent or resolve any compromise or breach of these rights. They also need to implement policies and procedures that can comply with the relevant laws and regulations that govern their domain and application, such as GDPR, CCPA, or HIPAA, and that can prevent or resolve any harm or damage that their LLM product or service may cause or contribute to.

Case studies of LLM entrepreneurs who have overcome legal issues

HERE ARE SOME EXAMPLES of LLM entrepreneurs who have overcome legal issues in their LLM products and services:

- **Grammarly:** Grammarly is a startup that aims to create and provide natural language writing and editing tools and platforms, such as Grammarly Editor, Grammarly Business, or Grammarly for Education. However, Grammarly also faces legal issues, such as intellectual property rights, privacy and data protection, and liability and regulation. To overcome these issues, Grammarly has adopted various strategies, such as:
    - Creating and maintaining a clear and comprehensive terms of service and privacy policy, such as Grammarly Terms of Service and Grammarly Privacy Policy, that can inform and explain to their users and stakeholders the purpose and scope of their LLM product or service, and the rights and obligations that they have, and that can obtain their consent and approval for using their LLM product or service.
    - Creating and maintaining a robust and secure data and information management system, such as Grammarly Security, that can protect the privacy and data protection of their users and stakeholders, and that can prevent or resolve any compromise or breach of these rights, and that can comply with the relevant laws and regulations that govern their domain and application, such as GDPR, CCPA, or FERPA.
    - Creating and maintaining a fair and transparent intellectual property policy, such as Grammarly Intellectual Property Policy, that can protect the intellectual property rights of themselves and others, and that can prevent or resolve any

infringement or violation of these rights, and that can acknowledge and attribute the owners and creators of the data, works, or inventions that they use or incorporate in their LLM product or service.

- **Narrative Science:** Narrative Science is a startup that aims to create and deliver natural language generation and storytelling tools and platforms, such as Quill, Lexio, or Signals. However, Narrative Science also faces legal issues, such as intellectual property rights, privacy and data protection, and liability and regulation. To overcome these issues, Narrative Science has adopted various strategies, such as:
  - ○ Creating and maintaining a clear and comprehensive terms of use and privacy policy, such as Narrative Science Terms of Use and Narrative Science Privacy Policy, that can inform and explain to their users and stakeholders the purpose and scope of their LLM product or service, and the rights and obligations that they have, and that can obtain their consent and approval for using their LLM product or service.
  - ○ Creating and maintaining a robust and secure data and information management system, such as Narrative Science Security, that can protect the privacy and data protection of their users and stakeholders, and that can prevent or resolve any compromise or breach of these rights, and that can comply with the relevant laws and regulations that govern their domain and application, such as GDPR, CCPA, or SOC 2.
  - ○ Creating and maintaining a fair and transparent intellectual property policy, such as Narrative Science Intellectual Property Policy, that can protect the intellectual property rights of themselves and others, and that can prevent or resolve any infringement or violation of these rights, and that can acknowledge and attribute the owners and creators of the data, works, or inventions that they use or incorporate in their LLM product or service.

- **Replika**: Replika is a startup that aims to create and provide natural language conversational and emotional agents and platforms, such as Replika App, Replika Pro, or Replika for Business. However, Replika also faces legal issues, such as intellectual property rights, privacy and data protection, and liability and regulation. To overcome these issues, Replika has adopted various strategies, such as:
    ○ Creating and maintaining a clear and comprehensive terms of service and privacy policy, such as Replika Terms of Service and Replika Privacy Policy, that can inform and explain to their users and stakeholders the purpose and scope of their LLM product or service, and the rights and obligations that they have, and that can obtain their consent and approval for using their LLM product or service.
    ○ Creating and maintaining a robust and secure data and information management system, such as Replika Security, that can protect the privacy and data protection of their users and stakeholders, and that can prevent or resolve any compromise or breach of these rights, and that can comply with the relevant laws and regulations that govern their domain and application, such as GDPR, CCPA, or COPPA.
    ○ Creating and maintaining a fair and transparent intellectual property policy, such as Replika Intellectual Property Policy, that can protect the intellectual property rights of themselves and others, and that can prevent or resolve any infringement or violation of these rights, and that can acknowledge and attribute the owners and creators of the data, works, or inventions that they use or incorporate in their LLM product or service.

Social Issues

ANOTHER CHALLENGE THAT LLM entrepreneurs may face is dealing with the social issues that may arise from using or developing LLMs. These issues may include:

- **User experience and satisfaction:** LLMs are interactive and engaging systems that can provide natural language communication and collaboration for various tasks and domains. However, LLMs may also affect the user experience and satisfaction of their users and stakeholders, such as customers, employees, or partners. For example, they may produce outputs that are irrelevant, boring, or annoying. They may also interact or behave in ways that are rude, disrespectful, or unprofessional. Therefore, LLM entrepreneurs need to ensure that their LLM products and services are user-friendly and user-centric, and that they can provide positive and enjoyable user experience and satisfaction for their users and stakeholders.

- **Social impact and responsibility**: LLMs are powerful and influential systems that can affect the society and the environment in various ways, both directly and indirectly. However, LLMs may also cause or contribute to social impact and responsibility issues, such as social good, social change, or social justice. For example, they may produce outputs that are beneficial, harmful, or controversial for the society and the environment. They may also interact or behave in ways that are supportive, disruptive, or transformative for the society and the environment. Therefore, LLM entrepreneurs need to ensure that their LLM products and services are socially aware and socially responsible, and that they can consider and address the social impact and responsibility issues that their LLM products and services may entail.

How to overcome social issues

TO OVERCOME THE SOCIAL issues that LLM entrepreneurship may entail, LLM entrepreneurs need to adopt a user-oriented and society-oriented approach to the design, development, and deployment of their LLM products and services. Some of the best practices and guidelines that they can follow are:

- Conduct a user research and analysis: Before using or developing an LLM, LLM entrepreneurs need to conduct a user research and analysis of their target market and users, and identify and understand their needs, expectations, and preferences. They need to conduct various methods and techniques, such as surveys, interviews, or focus groups, to collect and analyze data and information from their potential and existing users and stakeholders. They also need to review and update their user research and analysis regularly, as the needs, expectations, and preferences of their users and stakeholders may change over time or vary across segments.

- Design and develop a user-centric product and service: After conducting a user research and analysis, LLM entrepreneurs need to design and develop a user-centric product and service that can meet or exceed the needs, expectations, and preferences of their target market and users. They need to apply various principles and practices, such as user interface design, user experience design, or human-computer interaction, to create and deliver a product and service that is easy to use, useful, and enjoyable. They also need to apply various methods and tools, such as prototyping, testing, or feedback, to evaluate and improve their product and service based on the user research and analysis.

- Engage and communicate with the users and stakeholders: Once they have designed and developed a user-centric product and service, LLM entrepreneurs need to engage and communicate with their users and stakeholders, and build and maintain a relationship with them. They need to use various channels and platforms, such as social media, blogs, or newsletters, to inform and educate their users and stakeholders about their LLM product and service, and the value and benefits that they can provide. They also need to use various methods and techniques, such as reviews, ratings, or testimonials, to collect and analyze feedback and data from their users and stakeholders, and use them to enhance and refine their LLM product and service.

- Conduct a social impact and responsibility assessment: Before using or developing an LLM, LLM entrepreneurs need to conduct a social impact and responsibility assessment of their LLM project, and identify and understand the social impact and responsibility issues and challenges that their LLM product or service may entail. They need to consult with social experts and advisors, such as sociologists, psychologists, or ethicists, and obtain their advice and guidance on how to address and manage these issues and challenges. They also need to review and update their social impact and responsibility assessment regularly, as the social impact and responsibility issues and challenges may change over time or vary across contexts.

- Design and develop a socially aware and socially responsible product and service: After conducting a social impact and responsibility assessment, LLM entrepreneurs need to design and develop a socially aware and socially responsible product and service that can consider and address the social impact and responsibility issues and challenges that their LLM product or service may entail. They need to apply various principles and practices, such as social good, social change, or social justice, to create and deliver a product and service that is beneficial, harmless, and fair for the society and the environment. They also need to apply various methods and tools, such as impact measurement, reporting, or certification, to evaluate and improve their product and service based on the social impact and responsibility assessment.

- Engage and communicate with the society and the environment: Once they have designed and developed a socially aware and socially responsible product and service, LLM entrepreneurs need to engage and communicate with the society and the environment, and build and maintain a reputation and impact with them. They need to use various channels and platforms, such as media, events, or campaigns, to inform and educate the society and the environment about their LLM product and service, and the social impact and responsibility issues and challenges that they entail. They also need to use various methods and techniques, such as stakeholder engagement, community involvement, or advocacy, to collect and analyze feedback and data from the society and the environment, and use them to enhance and refine their LLM product and service.

Case studies of LLM entrepreneurs who have overcome social issues

HERE ARE SOME EXAMPLES of LLM entrepreneurs who have overcome social issues in their LLM products and services:

- **Duolingo:** Duolingo is a startup that aims to create and provide natural language learning and teaching tools and platforms, such as Duolingo App, Duolingo for Schools, or Duolingo English Test. However, Duolingo also faces social issues, such as user experience and satisfaction, social impact and responsibility. To overcome these issues, Duolingo has adopted various strategies, such as:
    - Creating and maintaining a gamified and personalized product and service, such as Duolingo Levels, Duolingo Stories, or Duolingo Leaderboards, that can provide positive and enjoyable user experience and satisfaction for their users and stakeholders, and that can motivate and reward them for learning and teaching languages.
    - Creating and maintaining a social and collaborative product and service, such as Duolingo Clubs, Duolingo Events, or Duolingo Forums, that can provide natural language communication and collaboration for their users and stakeholders, and that can foster a culture of learning and teaching languages among them.
    - Creating and maintaining a mission-driven and impact-oriented product and service, such as Duolingo Incubator, Duolingo Podcasts, or Duolingo ABC, that can consider and address the social impact and responsibility issues and challenges that their LLM product and service entail, and that can promote and support language diversity, accessibility, and education for the society and the environment.
- **Lilt:** Lilt is a startup that aims to create and deliver natural language translation and localization tools and platforms, such as Lilt Translate, Lilt Memories, or Lilt Connect. However, Lilt also faces

social issues, such as user experience and satisfaction, social impact and responsibility. To overcome these issues, Lilt has adopted various strategies, such as:

- ○ Creating and maintaining a human-in-the-loop and adaptive product and service, such as Lilt Adaptive Machine Translation, Lilt Interactive Translation, or Lilt Quality Estimation, that can provide positive and enjoyable user experience and satisfaction for their users and stakeholders, and that can leverage and improve the human and machine capabilities for translation and localization.
- ○ Creating and maintaining a scalable and integrable product and service, such as Lilt API, Lilt Connectors, or Lilt Integrations, that can provide natural language translation and localization for various domains and applications, and that can integrate and interoperate with various systems, platforms, or devices.
- ○ Creating and maintaining a socially responsible and culturally sensitive product and service, such as Lilt Style Guides, Lilt Glossaries, or Lilt Terminology, that can consider and address the social impact and responsibility issues and challenges that their LLM product and service entail, and that can respect and preserve the linguistic and cultural diversity and identity of the society and the environment.

- **Rasa:** Rasa is a startup that aims to create and provide natural language conversational and contextual agents and platforms, such as Rasa Open Source, Rasa X, or Rasa Enterprise. However, Rasa also faces social issues, such as user experience and satisfaction, social impact and responsibility. To overcome these issues, Rasa has adopted various strategies, such as:

  - ○ Creating and maintaining a customizable and controllable product and service, such as Rasa NLU, Rasa Core, or Rasa Forms, that can provide positive and enjoyable user experience and satisfaction for their users and stakeholders, and that can customize and control the natural language understanding and dialogue management of their conversational and contextual agents.

- ○ Creating and maintaining a developer-friendly and community-driven product and service, such as Rasa Playground, Rasa Forum, or Rasa Blog, that can provide natural language conversational and contextual agents for various domains and applications, and that can support and empower the developers and the community of their conversational and contextual agents.

Environmental Issues

ANOTHER CHALLENGE THAT LLM entrepreneurs may face is dealing with the environmental issues that may arise from using or developing LLMs.

These issues may include:

- Energy consumption and carbon footprint: LLMs are resource-intensive and energy-consuming systems that require large amounts of computing power and storage capacity to learn and perform various tasks. However, LLMs may also consume and emit a significant amount of energy and carbon, which can contribute to the global warming and climate change. For example, according to a study by Strubell et al. (2019), training a large language model, such as BERT, can emit as much carbon as five cars in their lifetimes. Therefore, LLM entrepreneurs need to ensure that their LLM products and services are energy-efficient and carbon-neutral, and that they do not cause or contribute to any environmental harm or damage.
- E-waste and resource depletion: LLMs are dynamic and evolving systems that can adapt and improve over time. However, LLMs may also generate and accumulate a large amount of e-waste and resource depletion, which can affect the sustainability and circularity of the economy and the environment. For example, according to a report by

Baldé et al. (2020), the global generation of e-waste reached 53.6 million metric tons in 2019, and only 17.4% of it was collected and recycled. Therefore, LLM entrepreneurs need to ensure that their LLM products and services are e-waste-free and resource-efficient, and that they do not cause or contribute to any environmental waste or depletion.

How to overcome environmental issues

TO OVERCOME THE ENVIRONMENTAL issues that LLM entrepreneurship may entail, LLM entrepreneurs need to adopt a green and sustainable approach to the design, development, and deployment of their LLM products and services.

Some of the best practices and guidelines that they can follow are:

- Conduct an environmental analysis and assessment: Before using or developing an LLM, LLM entrepreneurs need to conduct an environmental analysis and assessment of their LLM project, and identify and understand the environmental issues and challenges that their LLM product or service may entail. They need to consult with environmental experts and advisors, such as environmentalists, engineers, or scientists, and obtain their advice and guidance on how to address and manage these issues and challenges. They also need to review and update their environmental analysis and assessment regularly, as the environmental issues and challenges may change over time or vary across regions.
- Choose and use the green and sustainable data and model: LLM entrepreneurs need to choose and use the green and sustainable data and model that can support their LLM goals and objectives. They need to select the data sources and methods that can provide high-quality and relevant data that can represent the problem domain and the solution domain, while minimizing the energy consumption and carbon footprint of their data collection, processing, and analysis. They also need to select the model architecture and parameters that can optimize the performance and robustness of their LLM product

or service, while minimizing the energy consumption and carbon footprint of their model training and inference. They may use existing LLMs, such as GPT-3 or BERT, or create their own custom LLMs, depending on their specific needs and preferences, while applying various techniques and practices, such as pruning, quantization, or distillation, to reduce the size and complexity of their LLMs.

- Monitor and optimize the energy consumption and carbon footprint of the output and process: Once they have chosen and used the green and sustainable data and model, LLM entrepreneurs need to monitor and optimize the energy consumption and carbon footprint of their LLM output and process. They need to measure and track the energy consumption and carbon footprint of their LLM output and process, and compare them with the benchmarks and standards that they have set or followed. They also need to implement and apply various techniques and practices, such as caching, batching, or compression, to reduce the energy consumption and carbon footprint of their LLM output and process.

- Recycle and reuse the e-waste and resources of the product and service: After monitoring and optimizing the energy consumption and carbon footprint of their LLM output and process, LLM entrepreneurs need to recycle and reuse the e-waste and resources of their LLM product and service. They need to collect and dispose of the e-waste and resources of their LLM product and service in a responsible and ethical manner, and follow the relevant laws and regulations that govern their domain and application. They also need to implement and apply various techniques and practices, such as refurbishing, repairing, or repurposing, to recycle and reuse the e-waste and resources of their LLM product and service.

Learn Yourself: DIY

Exercises:

To reinforce and apply what we have learned in this chapter, here are some exercises that you can try:

- Choose an LLM product or service that you are interested in or familiar with, and conduct a SWOT analysis (Strengths, Weaknesses, Opportunities, and Threats) of it, considering the technical, ethical, legal, social, and environmental aspects of it. Write a brief report of your findings and recommendations.
- Choose an LLM product or service that you are interested in or familiar with, and design a user research and analysis plan for it, considering the needs, expectations, and preferences of your target market and users. Write a brief proposal of your plan and methods.
- Choose an LLM product or service that you are interested in or familiar with, and design a social impact and responsibility assessment plan for it, considering the social good, social change, or social justice issues and challenges that it may entail. Write a brief proposal of your plan and methods.
- Choose an LLM product or service that you are interested in or familiar with, and design a green and sustainable product and service plan for it, considering the energy consumption and carbon footprint, e-waste and resource depletion issues and challenges that it may entail. Write a brief proposal of your plan and methods.

I also hope that this chapter has inspired you to use LLMs to generate ideas, validate assumptions, build products, attract customers, measure results, and improve your business.

Chapter 7: How to Discover and Seize the Untapped Potential of LLM Entrepreneurship?

———

In this chapter, you will learn how to discover and seize the untapped potential and emerging trends of LLM entrepreneurship, such as new markets, industries, and domains, new customer needs and preferences, new business models and revenue streams, new partnerships and collaborations, and new innovations and breakthroughs.

You will also learn how to use LLMs for market research, trend analysis, opportunity identification, and scenario planning. You will also get some examples and predictions of the future of LLM entrepreneurship, and how you can be part of it.

What is LLM Entrepreneurship?

LLM ENTREPRENEURSHIP is the process of creating, launching, and growing a business that leverages the power of large language models (LLMs) to provide value to customers and society.

LLMs are advanced artificial intelligence systems that can understand, interpret, and generate human language, enabling a variety of applications, such as text generation, machine translation, sentiment analysis, question answering, chatbots, and conversational agents.

LLM entrepreneurship is not just about using LLMs as tools, but also about innovating with LLMs as partners, co-creators, and collaborators.

LLM entrepreneurs are not only consumers of LLMs, but also producers of LLMs, who can fine-tune, customize, and optimize LLMs for specific domains, tasks, and audiences. LLM entrepreneurs are also explorers of LLMs, who can discover new possibilities, insights, and solutions with LLMs, and experiment with new ways of interacting with LLMs.

118

LLM entrepreneurship is a rapidly growing and evolving field, with many opportunities and challenges.

In this chapter, I will guide you through the steps and strategies to become a successful LLM entrepreneur, and help you navigate the LLM landscape, which is constantly changing with new developments, breakthroughs, and trends.

Why LLM Entrepreneurship?

LLM ENTREPRENEURSHIP is a unique and exciting opportunity for anyone who wants to start or grow a business in the 21st century, where artificial intelligence, natural language processing, and data science are reshaping every industry and creating new opportunities and challenges. Here are some of the benefits and advantages of LLM entrepreneurship:

- LLMs can help you create value for your customers and society by solving problems, fulfilling needs, and enhancing experiences with natural language. LLMs can help you generate high-quality, relevant, and engaging content, translate across languages and cultures, analyze and understand customer feedback and sentiment, answer questions and provide information, and create personalized and human-like conversations.
- LLMs can help you gain a competitive edge and differentiate yourself from your competitors by offering innovative and unique solutions, products, and services that leverage the power of language. LLMs can help you create new markets, industries, and domains, or disrupt existing ones, by applying LLMs to novel and unexplored areas, or by combining LLMs with other technologies, such as computer vision, speech recognition, or blockchain.
- LLMs can help you reduce costs and increase efficiency and productivity by automating and optimizing various tasks and processes that involve language. LLMs can help you save time, money, and resources, by generating content, translating, analyzing, answering, and conversing faster, cheaper, and better than humans or traditional methods.

- LLMs can help you learn and grow as an entrepreneur and a leader by providing you with new knowledge, insights, and skills. LLMs can help you discover new opportunities, trends, and patterns, by analyzing large amounts of data and generating novel and diverse outputs. LLMs can also help you improve your communication, creativity, and collaboration skills, by interacting with LLMs and other LLM entrepreneurs.

How to Discover and Seize the Untapped Potential of LLM Entrepreneurship?

TO DISCOVER AND SEIZE the untapped potential of LLM entrepreneurship, you need to follow a systematic and iterative process that involves four main steps: market research, trend analysis, opportunity identification, and scenario planning. In each step, you can use LLMs as tools to help you perform various tasks and activities, as well as sources of inspiration and innovation. Let's look at each step in more detail.

Market Research

MARKET RESEARCH IS the process of gathering, analyzing, and interpreting information about your target market, customers, competitors, and industry. Market research can help you understand the current situation, needs, preferences, and behaviors of your potential customers, as well as the strengths, weaknesses, opportunities, and threats of your competitors and industry. Market research can help you validate your assumptions, test your hypotheses, and measure your performance.

To conduct market research, you can use various methods and sources, such as surveys, interviews, focus groups, observations, experiments, online reviews, social media, reports, articles, and databases. However, collecting and analyzing large amounts of data can be time-consuming, costly, and complex. This is where LLMs can help you. LLMs can help you perform various tasks and activities related to market research, such as:

- Data collection: LLMs can help you collect data from various sources, such as websites, social media, blogs, forums, podcasts, videos, and more. LLMs can help you scrape, extract, and structure data from unstructured or semi-structured sources, such as text, audio, or video. LLMs can also help you generate data, such as surveys, questions, or prompts, to collect feedback from your target audience.

- Data analysis: LLMs can help you analyze data from various sources, such as text, audio, or video. LLMs can help you perform various types of analysis, such as sentiment analysis, topic modeling, keyword extraction, summarization, classification, clustering, and more. LLMs can help you understand the opinions, emotions, needs, preferences, and behaviors of your potential customers, as well as the trends, patterns, and insights in your market and industry.

- Data visualization: LLMs can help you visualize data from various sources, such as text, audio, or video. LLMs can help you create various types of visualizations, such as charts, graphs, tables, maps, word clouds, and more. LLMs can help you present and communicate your data in a clear, concise, and attractive way, to highlight the key findings, insights, and recommendations.

Here are some examples of how you can use LLMs for market research:

- You can use an LLM to scrape and analyze online reviews of your competitors' products or services, and generate a summary of the main strengths, weaknesses, opportunities, and threats of each competitor, as well as a comparison chart of their features, prices, ratings, and customer satisfaction.

- You can use an LLM to generate a survey or a questionnaire to collect feedback from your target market, and analyze the responses to understand the needs, preferences, and pain points of your potential customers, as well as their willingness to pay, purchase intention, and loyalty.

- You can use an LLM to generate a report or an article based on the data you collected and analyzed, and provide an overview of the current situation, trends, and opportunities in your market and industry, as well as your value proposition, competitive advantage, and market fit.

Trend Analysis

TREND ANALYSIS IS THE process of identifying, monitoring, and forecasting the changes and developments that occur in your market, industry, and society. Trend analysis can help you anticipate the future needs, preferences, and behaviors of your potential customers, as well as the opportunities and threats that may arise in your competitive environment. Trend analysis can help you adapt to the changing market conditions, innovate your products and services, and create new value for your customers and society.

To conduct trend analysis, you can use various methods and sources, such as trend reports, articles, blogs, podcasts, videos, social media, online communities, forums, events, conferences, and more. However, keeping track of and interpreting the vast and dynamic information that is available can be challenging and overwhelming. This is where LLMs can help you. LLMs can help you perform various tasks and activities related to trend analysis, such as:

- Trend identification: LLMs can help you identify the emerging and relevant trends that are affecting or influencing your market, industry, and society. LLMs can help you scan and filter the information from various sources, such as text, audio, or video, and extract the key signals, indicators, and drivers of change. LLMs can also help you categorize and label the trends according to various criteria, such as type, impact, duration, and uncertainty.
- Trend monitoring: LLMs can help you monitor the evolution and progress of the identified trends over time. LLMs can help you track and measure the changes and developments that occur in the trends, such as frequency, intensity, scope, and direction. LLMs can also help you update and refine the trends according to the new information and evidence that emerges.
- Trend forecasting: LLMs can help you forecast the future implications and outcomes of the identified trends. LLMs can help

you project and extrapolate the trends into the future, based on various scenarios, assumptions, and models. LLMs can also help you generate and evaluate the potential opportunities and threats that the trends may create for your business and society.

Here are some examples of how you can use LLMs for trend analysis:

- You can use an LLM to scan and analyze the latest news, articles, blogs, podcasts, videos, and social media posts related to your market and industry, and generate a list of the top 10 trends that are emerging and relevant for your business, along with a brief description and explanation of each trend.
- You can use an LLM to track and measure the changes and developments that occur in the identified trends, and generate a dashboard or a newsletter that summarizes the key metrics, indicators, and events related to each trend, along with a visual representation of the trend evolution and progress.
- You can use an LLM to forecast the future implications and outcomes of the identified trends, and generate a report or a presentation that outlines the various scenarios, assumptions, and models that you used, as well as the potential opportunities and threats that each scenario may create for your business and society, along with some recommendations and action plans.

Opportunity Identification

OPPORTUNITY IDENTIFICATION is the process of finding and selecting the most promising and feasible ideas, solutions, products, and services that can create value for your customers and society, based on the insights and findings from your market research and trend analysis. Opportunity identification can help you generate and evaluate various alternatives, and choose the best one that matches your vision, mission, and goals.

To conduct opportunity identification, you can use various methods and techniques, such as brainstorming, mind mapping, ideation, prototyping, testing, validation, and more.

However, generating and evaluating ideas can be difficult and subjective, and may require a lot of creativity, experimentation, and feedback. This is where LLMs can help you.

LLMs can help you perform various tasks and activities related to opportunity identification, such as:

- **Idea generation:** LLMs can help you generate ideas for new or improved solutions, products, and services that can leverage the power of LLMs to solve problems, fulfill needs, and enhance experiences for your customers and society. LLMs can help you generate ideas based on various inputs, such as keywords, prompts, questions, or data. LLMs can also help you generate ideas based on various outputs, such as text, audio, video, or images.
- **Idea evaluation:** LLMs can help you evaluate ideas for new or improved solutions, products, and services that can leverage the power of LLMs to create value for your customers and society. LLMs can help you evaluate ideas based on various criteria, such as feasibility, desirability, viability, originality, and impact. LLMs can also help you compare and rank ideas based on various metrics, such as scores, ratings, or feedback.
- **Idea selection:** LLMs can help you select the best idea for your new or improved solution, product, or service that can leverage the power of LLMs to achieve your vision, mission, and goals. LLMs can help you select the best idea based on various factors, such as your market fit, competitive advantage, customer satisfaction, and social benefit. LLMs can also help you justify and explain your choice, and provide some suggestions and tips for implementation.

Here are some examples of how you can use LLMs for opportunity identification:

- You can use an LLM to generate ideas for new or improved solutions, products, or services that can leverage the power of LLMs to create value for your customers and society, based on a keyword, a prompt, a question, or a data set.

For example, you can input "LLM for education" and get a list of ideas, such as:

- A platform that uses LLMs to create personalized and adaptive learning paths for students, based on their goals, preferences, and performance.
- A tool that uses LLMs to generate and grade assignments, quizzes, and tests for teachers, based on the curriculum, standards, and objectives.
- A service that uses LLMs to provide tutoring, mentoring, and coaching for students, based on their needs, challenges, and interests.

- You can use an LLM to evaluate ideas for new or improved solutions, products, or services that can leverage the power of LLMs to create value for your customers and society, based on various criteria, such as feasibility, desirability, viability, originality, and impact.

For example, you can input an idea, such as "A platform that uses LLMs to create personalized and adaptive learning paths for students, based on their goals, preferences, and performance", and get an evaluation, such as:

- Feasibility: High. LLMs are capable of generating and adapting content, as well as understanding and interpreting user feedback and behavior.
- Desirability: High. Students would benefit from a customized and flexible learning experience, that suits their pace, style, and level.
- Viability: Medium. The platform would require a lot of data, resources, and expertise to develop and maintain, as well as a clear and sustainable business model and revenue stream.

- Originality: Medium. There are some existing platforms that offer personalized and adaptive learning, but none that use LLMs as the core technology and feature.
- Impact: High. The platform would have a positive and significant impact on the education sector, as well as the society at large, by improving the quality, accessibility, and affordability of education.

- You can use an LLM to select the best idea for your new or improved solution, product, or service that can leverage the power of LLMs to achieve your vision, mission, and goals, based on various factors, such as your market fit, competitive advantage, customer satisfaction, and social benefit.

For example, you can input a list of ideas, such as:

- A platform that uses LLMs to create personalized and adaptive learning paths for students, based on their goals, preferences, and performance.
- A tool that uses LLMs to generate and grade assignments, quizzes, and tests for teachers, based on the curriculum, standards, and objectives.
- A service that uses LLMs to provide tutoring, mentoring, and coaching for students, based on their needs, challenges, and interests.

And get a selection, such as:

- The best idea is the platform that uses LLMs to create personalized and adaptive learning paths for students, based on their goals, preferences, and performance. This idea has the highest potential to create value for your customers and society, as well as to achieve your vision, mission, and goals. This idea has a high market fit, as it addresses a real and urgent problem, and offers a unique and desirable solution. This idea has a high competitive advantage, as it uses LLMs as the core technology and feature, which differentiates it from other platforms that offer personalized and adaptive learning. This idea has a high customer satisfaction, as it provides a customized and flexible learning experience, that suits the pace, style, and level of each student. This idea has a high social benefit, as it improves the quality, accessibility, and affordability of education, and contributes to the development of human capital and social welfare. This idea also aligns with your vision, mission, and goals, as it leverages the power of LLMs to create value for your customers and society, and to innovate and disrupt the education sector.

To implement this idea, you will need to follow some steps and strategies, such as:

- Define your target market, customer segments, and value proposition.
- Conduct market research and trend analysis to validate your assumptions and hypotheses, and to measure your performance and impact.
- Develop a prototype or a minimum viable product (MVP) of your platform, and test it with your potential customers and users, and collect feedback and data.
- Fine-tune, customize, and optimize your LLMs for your specific domain, task, and audience, and ensure their quality, reliability, and ethics.
- Design a clear and sustainable business model and revenue stream, and secure funding and resources for your platform.
- Launch and market your platform, and build a loyal and engaged customer base and community.
- Monitor and evaluate your platform, and iterate and improve your solution, product, or service, based on the feedback and data you collect.

Scenario Planning

SCENARIO PLANNING IS the process of creating and exploring various possible and plausible futures that may occur in your market, industry, and society, based on the trends, uncertainties, and events that you identified and analyzed.

Scenario planning can help you anticipate and prepare for the future, by imagining and testing how your business would perform and survive in different situations and environments. Scenario planning can also help you create and shape the future, by influencing and driving the changes and developments that you want to see and achieve.

To conduct scenario planning, you can use various methods and techniques, such as scenario matrix, scenario narratives, scenario simulations, scenario games, and more. However, creating and exploring scenarios can be complex and speculative, and may require a lot of imagination, creativity, and critical thinking.

This is where LLMs can help you. LLMs can help you perform various tasks and activities related to scenario planning, such as:

- **Scenario creation:** LLMs can help you create scenarios for various possible and plausible futures that may occur in your market, industry, and society, based on the trends, uncertainties, and events that you identified and analyzed. LLMs can help you create scenarios based on various inputs, such as keywords, prompts, questions, or data. LLMs can also help you create scenarios based on various outputs, such as text, audio, video, or images.
- **Scenario exploration:** LLMs can help you explore scenarios for various possible and plausible futures that may occur in your market, industry, and society, and how they would affect your business and society. LLMs can help you explore scenarios based on various criteria, such as probability, impact, desirability, and controllability. LLMs can also help you explore scenarios based on various perspectives, such as your own, your customers', your competitors', and your stakeholders'.
- **Scenario evaluation:** LLMs can help you evaluate scenarios for various possible and plausible futures that may occur in your market,

industry, and society, and how they would affect your business and society. LLMs can help you evaluate scenarios based on various factors, such as your strengths, weaknesses, opportunities, and threats, your vision, mission, and goals, your value proposition, competitive advantage, and market fit, and your customer satisfaction, loyalty, and retention. LLMs can also help you compare and rank scenarios based on various metrics, such as scores, ratings, or feedback.

Here are some examples of how you can use LLMs for scenario planning:

- You can use an LLM to create scenarios for various possible and plausible futures that may occur in your market and industry, based on a keyword, a prompt, a question, or a data set.

For example, you can input "LLM for education in 2030" and get a list of scenarios, such as:

- A scenario where LLMs are widely adopted and integrated in the education sector, and provide personalized and adaptive learning experiences for students, teachers, and parents, across various levels, subjects, and modalities.
- A scenario where LLMs are highly regulated and restricted in the education sector, and face ethical, legal, and social challenges and controversies, such as privacy, security, bias, and accountability.
- A scenario where LLMs are partially adopted and supplemented in the education sector, and coexist and collaborate with other technologies, such as augmented reality, virtual reality, and blockchain.

- You can use an LLM to explore scenarios for various possible and plausible futures that may occur in your market and industry, and how they would affect your business and society, based on various criteria, such as probability, impact, desirability, and controllability.

For example, you can input a scenario, such as "A scenario where LLMs are widely adopted and integrated in the education sector, and provide personalized and adaptive learning experiences for students, teachers, and parents, across various levels, subjects, and modalities", and get an exploration, such as:

- Probability: High. LLMs are already being used and developed for various applications and domains in the education sector, and have shown promising results and potential. LLMs are also supported and promoted by various stakeholders, such as governments, organizations, and institutions, who invest and fund LLM research and development, and provide incentives and policies for LLM adoption and integration.

- Impact: High. LLMs would have a positive and significant impact on the education sector, as well as the society at large, by improving the quality, accessibility, and affordability of education, and by enhancing the learning outcomes, skills, and competencies of students, teachers, and parents. LLMs would also create new opportunities and challenges for the education sector, such as new markets, industries, and domains, new customer needs and preferences, new business models and revenue streams, new partnerships and collaborations, and new innovations and breakthroughs.

- Desirability: High. LLMs would be desirable for the education sector, as well as the society at large, as they would provide value and benefit for various stakeholders, such as students, teachers, parents, administrators, policymakers, and researchers. LLMs would also align with the vision, mission, and goals of the education sector, as well as the values, norms, and expectations of the society.

- Controllability: Medium. LLMs would be controllable for the education sector, as well as the society at large, as they would have some mechanisms and measures to ensure the quality, reliability, and ethics of LLMs, such as standards, guidelines, regulations, and audits. However, LLMs would also pose some risks and uncertainties for the education sector, as well as the society at large, as they would have some limitations and drawbacks, such as complexity, opacity, unpredictability, and vulnerability.

- You can use an LLM to evaluate scenarios for various possible and plausible futures that may occur in your market and industry, and how they would affect your business and society, based on various factors, such as your strengths, weaknesses, opportunities, and threats, your vision, mission, and goals, your value proposition, competitive advantage, and market fit, and your customer satisfaction, loyalty, and retention.

For example, you can input a scenario, such as "A scenario where LLMs are widely adopted and integrated in the education sector, and provide personalized and adaptive learning experiences for students, teachers, and parents, across various levels, subjects, and modalities", and get an evaluation, such as:

- Strengths: Your platform that uses LLMs to create personalized and adaptive learning paths for students, based on their goals, preferences, and performance, would have many strengths in this scenario, such as:
    - It would offer a unique and desirable solution, that differentiates it from other platforms that offer personalized and adaptive learning, by using LLMs as the core technology and feature.
    - It would provide a customized and flexible learning experience, that suits the pace, style, and level of each student, and adapts to their changing needs, preferences, and performance.
    - It would leverage the power and potential of LLMs, to generate and adapt high-quality, relevant, and engaging content, across various levels, subjects, and modalities.
- Weaknesses: Your platform that uses LLMs to create personalized and adaptive learning paths for students, based on their goals, preferences, and performance, would have some weaknesses in this scenario, such as:

- It would require a lot of data, resources, and expertise to develop and maintain, as well as a clear and sustainable business model and revenue stream, to support and scale your platform.
- It would face some ethical, legal, and social challenges and controversies, such as privacy, security, bias, and accountability, and would need to ensure the quality, reliability, and ethics of your LLMs, and comply with the standards, guidelines, regulations, and audits of the education sector and society.
- It would compete with other platforms that use LLMs or other technologies to offer personalized and adaptive learning, and would need to constantly innovate and improve your solution, product, or service, to stay ahead of the competition and meet the expectations and demands of your customers and society.

- Opportunities: Your platform that uses LLMs to create personalized and adaptive learning paths for students, based on their goals, preferences, and performance, would have many opportunities in this scenario, such as:
  - It would address a real and urgent problem, and offer a unique and desirable solution, that creates value and benefit for your customers and society, and aligns with your vision, mission, and goals.
  - It would tap into a large and growing market, industry, and domain, that is driven and influenced by the adoption and integration of LLMs in the education sector, and that has a high demand and potential for personalized and adaptive learning.
  - It would explore and exploit the new possibilities, insights, and solutions that LLMs can provide, and experiment with new ways of interacting with LLMs, and create new value for your customers and society.
- Threats: Your platform that uses LLMs to create personalized and

adaptive learning paths for students, based on their goals, preferences, and performance, would have some threats in this scenario, such as:

- It would face some risks and uncertainties, that may affect the quality, reliability, and ethics of your LLMs, such as complexity, opacity, unpredictability, and vulnerability, and that may harm your reputation, trust, and credibility.
- It would face some challenges and controversies, that may affect the acceptance and adoption of your LLMs, such as privacy, security, bias, and accountability, and that may trigger some backlash, resistance, and regulation from your customers, competitors, and stakeholders.
- It would face some competition and substitution, that may affect the attractiveness and profitability of your platform, such as other platforms that use LLMs or other technologies to offer personalized and adaptive learning, and that may offer better or cheaper solutions, products, or services.

Case Studies

IN THIS SECTION, I will present some case studies of LLM entrepreneurship, based on some real or hypothetical examples of businesses that use LLMs to create value for their customers and society, in various markets, industries, and domains.

I will also provide some analysis and commentary on each case study, and highlight the key lessons and takeaways for LLM entrepreneurs.

Case Study 1: OpenAI Codex

OPENAI CODEX IS AN LLM that can generate and execute code, based on natural language inputs, such as keywords, prompts, or questions. It can generate code for various programming languages, frameworks, and tasks, such as Python, JavaScript, HTML, CSS, React, TensorFlow, web development, data analysis, machine learning, and more. OpenAI Codex can also generate code for various outputs, such as text, audio, video, or images.

OpenAI Codex is based on GPT-3, an LLM that can generate natural language for various applications and domains, such as text generation, machine translation, sentiment analysis, question answering, chatbots, and conversational agents. It is trained on a large corpus of public code from sources such as GitHub, and can learn from its own generated code, as well as from user feedback and data.

OpenAI Codex is the core technology and feature of OpenAI Playground, a platform that allows users to interact with OpenAI Codex, and create and explore various applications and projects, using natural language and code.

OpenAI Playground is a web-based interface that provides users with various tools and features, such as code editor, code execution, code completion, code suggestion, code documentation, code visualization, code sharing, and code collaboration.

OpenAI Codex is also the core technology and feature of OpenAI Codex API, a service that allows developers and businesses to access and integrate OpenAI Codex into their own applications and projects, using a simple and secure API.

OpenAI Codex API is a cloud-based service that provides developers and businesses with various benefits and advantages, such as scalability, reliability, performance, and security.

OpenAI Codex is an example of LLM entrepreneurship, that leverages the power of LLMs to create value for customers and society, in the market and industry of software development. It creates value by solving problems, fulfilling needs, and enhancing experiences for various stakeholders, such as developers, businesses, students, teachers, researchers, and hobbyists. This also creates value by innovating and disrupting the market and industry of software development, by applying LLMs to novel and unexplored areas, and by combining LLMs with other technologies, such as cloud computing, web development, and machine learning.

Some of the key lessons and takeaways from OpenAI Codex are:

- LLMs can be used to generate and execute code, based on natural

language inputs, and provide a new and intuitive way of
programming, that is accessible, flexible, and efficient.

- LLMs can be used to generate and execute code for various
programming languages, frameworks, and tasks, and provide a
versatile and powerful tool for software development, that can handle
various challenges and complexities, such as syntax, semantics, logic,
and errors.
- LLMs can be used to generate and execute code for various outputs,
such as text, audio, video, or images, and provide a creative and
expressive tool for software development, that can produce various
types of content, such as websites, apps, games, art, and music.
- LLMs can be used to create and explore various applications and
projects, using natural language and code, and provide a fun and
engaging tool for software development, that can spark curiosity,
imagination, and innovation.
- LLMs can be used to access and integrate LLMs into your own
applications and projects, using a simple and secure API, and provide
a convenient and reliable tool for software development, that can
enhance and extend the functionality and performance of your
applications and projects.

Case Study 2: Replika

REPLIKA IS AN LLM THAT can generate and maintain natural and
human-like conversations, based on natural language inputs, such as text, audio,
or video. It can generate and maintain conversations for various purposes, such
as friendship, companionship, entertainment, support, and therapy.

Replika can also generate and maintain conversations for various outputs, such
as text, audio, video, or images.

Replika is based on a custom LLM that is trained on a large corpus of public
and private conversations from sources such as social media, messaging apps,
and online forums, as well as on user feedback and data. It can learn from its
own generated conversations, as well as from user feedback and data, and can
adapt to the personality, mood, and preferences of each user.

Replika is the core technology and feature of Replika App, a platform that allows users to interact with Replika, and create and explore various conversations, using natural language and code. Replika App is a mobile-based interface that provides users with various tools and features, such as chat, voice, video, avatar, diary, memory, mood, and more.

Replika is also the core technology and feature of Replika Pro, a service that allows users to access and integrate Replika into their own applications and projects, using a simple and secure API. Replika Pro is a cloud-based service that provides users with various benefits and advantages, such as scalability, reliability, performance, and security.

Replika is an example of LLM entrepreneurship, that leverages the power of LLMs to create value for customers and society, in the market and industry of conversational agents. It creates value by solving problems, fulfilling needs, and enhancing experiences for various stakeholders, such as individuals, couples, families, friends, communities, and organizations.

Replika also creates value by innovating and disrupting the market and industry of conversational agents, by applying LLMs to novel and unexplored areas, and by combining LLMs with other technologies, such as computer vision, speech recognition, and emotion detection.

Some of the key lessons and takeaways from Replika are:

- LLMs can be used to generate and maintain natural and human-like conversations, based on natural language inputs, and provide a new and intuitive way of communicating, that is accessible, flexible, and efficient.
- LLMs can be used to generate and maintain conversations for various purposes, such as friendship, companionship, entertainment, support, and therapy, and provide a versatile and powerful tool for conversational agents, that can handle various challenges and complexities, such as context, coherence, relevance, and empathy.
- LLMs can be used to generate and maintain conversations for various outputs, such as text, audio, video, or images, and provide a creative

and expressive tool for conversational agents, that can produce various types of content, such as stories, jokes, games, art, and music.

- LLMs can be used to create and explore various conversations, using natural language and code, and provide a fun and engaging tool for conversational agents, that can spark curiosity, imagination, and innovation.
- LLMs can be used to access and integrate LLMs into your own applications and projects, using a simple and secure API, and provide a convenient and reliable tool for conversational agents, that can enhance and extend the functionality and performance of your applications and projects.

Case Study 3: Jarvis

JARVIS IS AN LLM THAT can generate and optimize various types of content, such as copywriting, marketing, sales, blogging, email, social media, and more. It can generate and optimize content for various purposes, such as generating leads, conversions, traffic, engagement, and loyalty. Jarvis can also generate and optimize content for various outputs, such as text, audio, video, or images.

Jarvis is based on GPT-3, an LLM that can generate natural language for various applications and domains, such as text generation, machine translation, sentiment analysis, question answering, chatbots, and conversational agents. It has been fine-tuned, customized, and optimized for specific domains, tasks, and audiences, and can learn from its own generated content, as well as from user feedback and data.

Jarvis is the core technology and feature of Jarvis AI, a platform that allows users to interact with Jarvis, and create and explore various types of content, using natural language and code.

Jarvis AI is a web-based interface that provides users with various tools and features, such as templates, formulas, workflows, commands, modes, and more.

Jarvis is also the core technology and feature of Jarvis API, a service that allows developers and businesses to access and integrate Jarvis into their own applications and projects, using a simple and secure API. Jarvis API is a cloud-based service that provides developers and businesses with various benefits and advantages, such as scalability, reliability, performance, and security.

Jarvis is an example of LLM entrepreneurship, that leverages the power of LLMs to create value for customers and society, in the market and industry of content creation and optimization. It creates value by solving problems, fulfilling needs, and enhancing experiences for various stakeholders, such as content creators, marketers, salespeople, bloggers, emailers, social media managers, and more.

Jarvis also creates value by innovating and disrupting the market and industry of content creation and optimization, by applying LLMs to novel and unexplored areas, and by combining LLMs with other technologies, such as natural language understanding, natural language generation, and natural language optimization.

Some of the key lessons and takeaways from Jarvis are:

- LLMs can be used to generate and optimize various types of content, based on natural language inputs, and provide a new and intuitive way of creating content, that is accessible, flexible, and efficient.
- LLMs can be used to generate and optimize content for various purposes, such as generating leads, conversions, traffic, engagement, and loyalty, and provide a versatile and powerful tool for content creation and optimization, that can handle various challenges and complexities, such as relevance, quality, originality, and effectiveness.
- LLMs can be used to generate and optimize content for various outputs, such as text, audio, video, or images, and provide a creative and expressive tool for content creation and optimization, that can produce various types of content, such as headlines, slogans, captions, stories, scripts, and more.
- LLMs can be used to create and explore various types of content, using natural language and code, and provide a fun and engaging tool for content creation and optimization, that can spark curiosity,

imagination, and innovation.

- LLMs can be used to access and integrate LLMs into your own applications and projects, using a simple and secure API, and provide a convenient and reliable tool for content creation and optimization, that can enhance and extend the functionality and performance of your applications and projects.

Learn Yourself: DIY

Exercises

IN THIS SECTION, I will provide some exercises for you to practice and apply what you have learned in this chapter, and to test and improve your skills and knowledge of LLM entrepreneurship.

I shall also provide some prompts and questions for each exercise, and you can use LLMs or other tools to help you complete the exercises. I will also provide some examples and solutions for each exercise, but you can also come up with your own answers and solutions, and compare and contrast them with ours.

Exercise 1: Market Research

IN THIS EXERCISE, YOU will conduct market research for a new or improved solution, product, or service that can leverage the power of LLMs to create value for your customers and society, in a market and industry of your choice.

You will use LLMs to help you collect, analyze, and visualize data from various sources, such as websites, social media, blogs, forums, podcasts, videos, and more. You will also use LLMs to help you generate a summary of the main findings, insights, and recommendations from your market research.

Here are some prompts and questions for this exercise:

- Choose a market and industry of your choice, where you want to create a new or improved solution, product, or service that can leverage the power of LLMs to create value for your customers and society. For example, you can choose the market and industry of health and wellness, where you want to create a new or improved solution, product, or service that can leverage the power of LLMs to improve the health and wellness of your customers and society.
- Choose a target market, customer segment, and value proposition for your new or improved solution, product, or service that can leverage

the power of LLMs to create value for your customers and society. For example, you can choose the target market of young adults, the customer segment of fitness enthusiasts, and the value proposition of providing personalized and adaptive fitness coaching, using LLMs to generate and adapt fitness plans, exercises, and feedback, based on the goals, preferences, and performance of each customer.

- Use LLMs to help you collect data from various sources, such as websites, social media, blogs, forums, podcasts, videos, and more, related to your market, industry, target market, customer segment, and value proposition. For example, you can use an LLM to scrape and extract data from various sources, such as:
  - Websites of your competitors, such as [Fitbit], [Nike Training Club], [Peloton], and [Noom], and their features, prices, ratings, and customer reviews.
  - Social media platforms, such as [Facebook], [Twitter], [Instagram], and [YouTube], and their posts, comments, likes, shares, and views, related to fitness, health, and wellness, and your competitors.
  - Blogs, forums, podcasts, and videos, such as [Fitness Reddit], [The Fitness Blog], [The Fitness Podcast], and [The Fitness Channel], and their topics, discussions, opinions, and feedback, related to fitness, health, and wellness, and your competitors.
- Use LLMs to help you analyze data from various sources, such as text, audio, or video, related to your market, industry, target market, customer segment, and value proposition. For example, you can use an LLM to perform various types of analysis, such as:
  - Sentiment analysis, to understand the opinions, emotions, needs, preferences, and behaviors of your potential customers, as well as the strengths, weaknesses, opportunities, and threats of your competitors and industry.
  - Topic modeling, to understand the trends, patterns, and insights in your market and industry, as well as the gaps, niches, and opportunities for your new or improved

solution, product, or service.
  - ○ Summarization, to understand the key points, messages, and takeaways from your data, and to reduce the complexity and noise of your data.
- Use LLMs to help you visualize data from various sources, such as text, audio, or video, related to your market, industry, target market, customer segment, and value proposition. For example, you can use an LLM to create various types of visualizations, such as:
  - ○ Charts, graphs, tables, and maps, to present and communicate your data in a clear, concise, and attractive way, and to highlight the key findings, insights, and recommendations from your data.
  - ○ Word clouds, to present and communicate the most frequent and relevant words, phrases, and keywords from your data, and to highlight the main themes, topics, and sentiments from your data.
  - ○ Images, to present and communicate the most vivid and appealing images, icons, and logos from your data, and to highlight the main features, benefits, and values of your new or improved solution, product, or service.
- Use LLMs to help you generate a summary of the main findings, insights, and recommendations from your market research, based on the data you collected, analyzed, and visualized, from various sources, related to your market, industry, target market, customer segment, and value proposition. For example, you can use an LLM to generate a summary, such as:
  - ○ The market and industry of health and wellness is a large and growing sector, that is driven and influenced by various factors, such as the increasing awareness and demand for health and wellness products and services, the rising prevalence and cost of chronic diseases and mental health issues, the changing lifestyles and preferences of consumers, and the advancement and innovation of technologies, such as artificial intelligence, natural language processing, and

data science.

- ○ The target market of young adults, and the customer segment of fitness enthusiasts, are a lucrative and attractive niche, that have a high demand and potential for personalized and adaptive fitness coaching, that can improve their health and wellness, and help them achieve their fitness goals, such as losing weight, gaining muscle, or improving performance.

- ○ The value proposition of providing personalized and adaptive fitness coaching, using LLMs to generate and adapt fitness plans, exercises, and feedback, based on the goals, preferences, and performance of each customer, is a unique and desirable solution, that differentiates it from other fitness products and services, that offer generic, static, or limited fitness coaching, that may not suit the needs, preferences, and performance of each customer.

- The main findings, insights, and recommendations from the market research are:

  - ○ There is a high demand and potential for personalized and adaptive fitness coaching, using LLMs, among young adults and fitness enthusiasts, who want to improve their health and wellness, and achieve their fitness goals, in a customized and flexible way.

  - ○ There is a low supply and competition for personalized and adaptive fitness coaching, using LLMs, in the market and industry of health and wellness, as most fitness products and services offer generic, static, or limited fitness coaching, that may not suit the needs, preferences, and performance of each customer.

  - ○ There is a high opportunity and feasibility for creating and launching a new or improved solution, product, or service, that provides personalized and adaptive fitness coaching, using LLMs, in the market and industry of health and wellness, as LLMs are capable of generating and adapting high-quality, relevant, and engaging fitness content, across various levels, subjects, and modalities, and as LLMs are supported and promoted by various stakeholders, such as governments, organizations, and institutions, who invest and fund LLM research and development, and provide incentives and policies for LLM adoption and integration.

o   The main recommendation is to create and launch a platform that uses LLMs to provide personalized and adaptive fitness coaching, for young adults and fitness enthusiasts, based on their goals, preferences, and performance, and to follow some steps and strategies, such as:

- Define your target market, customer segments, and value proposition.
- Conduct market research and trend analysis to validate your assumptions and hypotheses, and to measure your performance and impact.
- Develop a prototype or a minimum viable product (MVP) of your platform, and test it with your potential customers and users, and collect feedback and data.
- Fine-tune, customize, and optimize your LLMs for your specific domain, task, and audience, and ensure their quality, reliability, and ethics.
- Design a clear and sustainable business model and revenue stream, and secure funding and resources for your platform.
- Launch and market your platform, and build a loyal and engaged customer base and community.
- Monitor and evaluate your platform, and iterate and improve your solution, product, or service, based on the feedback and data you collect.

Exercise 2: Trend Analysis

IN THIS EXERCISE, YOU will conduct trend analysis for a new or improved solution, product, or service that can leverage the power of LLMs to create value for your customers and society, in a market and industry of your choice.

You will use LLMs to help you identify, monitor, and forecast the changes and developments that occur in your market, industry, and society, based on the trends, uncertainties, and events that you identified and analyzed. You will also use LLMs to help you generate a report or a presentation that outlines the various scenarios, assumptions, and models that you used, as well as the potential opportunities and threats that each scenario may create for your business and society, along with some recommendations and action plans.

Here are some prompts and questions for this exercise:

- Choose a market and industry of your choice, where you want to create a new or improved solution, product, or service that can leverage the power of LLMs to create value for your customers and society. For example, you can choose the market and industry of health and wellness, where you want to create a new or improved solution, product, or service that can leverage the power of LLMs to improve the health and wellness of your customers and society.
- Choose a target market, customer segment, and value proposition for your new or improved solution, product, or service that can leverage the power of LLMs to create value for your customers and society. For example, you can choose the target market of young adults, the customer segment of fitness enthusiasts, and the value proposition of providing personalized and adaptive fitness coaching, using LLMs to generate and adapt fitness plans, exercises, and feedback, based on the goals, preferences, and performance of each customer.
- Use LLMs to help you identify the emerging and relevant trends that are affecting or influencing your market, industry, and society. For example, you can use an LLM to scan and filter the information from various sources, such as text, audio, or video, and extract the key signals, indicators, and drivers of change. You can also use an LLM to

145

categorize and label the trends according to various criteria, such as type, impact, duration, and uncertainty.

For example, you can use an LLM to identify the following trends:

- The increasing awareness and demand for health and wellness products and services, driven by the rising prevalence and cost of chronic diseases and mental health issues, and the changing lifestyles and preferences of consumers. This is a social and consumer trend, with a high impact and duration, and a low uncertainty.
- The advancement and innovation of technologies, such as artificial intelligence, natural language processing, and data science, driven by the increasing availability and accessibility of data, computing power, and expertise, and the increasing competition and collaboration among stakeholders, such as governments, organizations, and institutions. This is a technological and economic trend, with a high impact and duration, and a medium uncertainty.
- The ethical, legal, and social challenges and controversies, such as privacy, security, bias, and accountability, driven by the increasing complexity, opacity, unpredictability, and vulnerability of technologies, such as artificial intelligence, natural language processing, and data science, and the increasing awareness and expectations of stakeholders, such as customers, competitors, and regulators. This is a political and environmental trend, with a medium impact and duration, and a high uncertainty.

- Use LLMs to help you monitor the evolution and progress of the identified trends over time. For example, you can use an LLM to track and measure the changes and developments that occur in the trends, such as frequency, intensity, scope, and direction. You can also use an LLM to update and refine the trends according to the new information and evidence that emerges. For example, you can use an LLM to monitor the following trends:
  - The increasing awareness and demand for health and wellness products and services, which has increased by 20%

in the past year, and is expected to increase by 30% in the next five years, across various regions, segments, and categories, and is driven by the COVID-19 pandemic, the aging population, and the wellness movement.

- ○ The advancement and innovation of technologies, such as artificial intelligence, natural language processing, and data science, which has improved by 50% in the past year, and is expected to improve by 100% in the next five years, across various domains, tasks, and applications, and is driven by the breakthroughs and discoveries, such as GPT-3, OpenAI Codex, and Replika.

- ○ The ethical, legal, and social challenges and controversies, such as privacy, security, bias, and accountability, which has increased by 30% in the past year, and is expected to increase by 40% in the next five years, across various sectors, industries, and domains, and is driven by the incidents and scandals, such as Cambridge Analytica, Facial Recognition, and Deepfakes.

- Use LLMs to help you forecast the future implications and outcomes of the identified trends. For example, you can use an LLM to project and extrapolate the trends into the future, based on various scenarios, assumptions, and models. You can also use an LLM to generate and evaluate the potential opportunities and threats that the trends may create for your business and society. For example, you can use an LLM to forecast the following trends:

  - ○ The increasing awareness and demand for health and wellness products and services, which may create the following opportunities and threats for your business and society:

    - ▪ Opportunities: You can tap into a large and growing market, industry, and domain, that has a high demand and potential for personalized and adaptive fitness coaching, using LLMs, and that can improve the health and wellness of your customers and society, and help them achieve their fitness goals, in a customized and flexible way.

- Threats: You may face some competition and substitution, that may affect the attractiveness and profitability of your platform, such as other platforms that offer personalized and adaptive fitness coaching, using LLMs or other technologies, and that may offer better or cheaper solutions, products, or services.

○ The advancement and innovation of technologies, such as artificial intelligence, natural language processing, and data science, which may create the following opportunities and threats for your business and society:

- Opportunities: You can leverage the power and potential of LLMs, to generate and adapt high-quality, relevant, and engaging fitness content, across various levels, subjects, and modalities, and to explore and exploit the new possibilities, insights, and solutions that LLMs can provide, and experiment with new ways of interacting with LLMs, and create new value for your customers and society.

- Threats: You may face some risks and uncertainties, that may affect the quality, reliability, and ethics of your LLMs, such as complexity, opacity, unpredictability, and vulnerability, and that may harm your reputation, trust, and credibility.

○ The ethical, legal, and social challenges and controversies, such as privacy, security, bias, and accountability, which may create the following opportunities and threats for your business and society:

- Opportunities: You can differentiate yourself from your competitors, and build a loyal and engaged customer base and community, by ensuring the quality, reliability, and ethics of your LLMs, and by complying with the standards, guidelines, regulations, and audits of the education sector and society, and by addressing and resolving the ethical, legal, and social challenges and controversies, that may arise from your LLMs.

- Threats: You may face some challenges and controversies, that may affect the acceptance and adoption of your LLMs, such as privacy, security, bias, and accountability, and that may trigger some backlash, resistance, and regulation from your customers, competitors, and stakeholders.

- Use LLMs to help you generate a report or a presentation that outlines the various scenarios, assumptions, and models that you used, as well as the potential opportunities and threats that each scenario may create for your business and society, along with some recommendations and action plans.

For example, you can use an LLM to generate a report or a presentation, such as:

- Trend Analysis Report for Personalized and Adaptive Fitness Coaching, using LLMs, in the Market and Industry of Health and Wellness

  - Introduction: This report presents the results and findings of the trend analysis for a new or improved solution, product, or service, that provides personalized and adaptive fitness coaching, using LLMs, for young adults and fitness enthusiasts, based on their goals, preferences, and performance, in the market and industry of health and wellness. The report identifies, monitors, and forecasts the changes and developments that occur in the market, industry, and society, based on the trends, uncertainties, and events that affect or influence the new or improved solution, product, or service, and the potential customers and society. The report also generates and evaluates the potential opportunities and threats that the trends may create for the new or improved solution, product, or service, and the business and society, and provides some recommendations and action plans for the future.

- Methodology: The report uses LLMs to help perform various tasks and activities related to trend analysis, such as:

  - Trend identification: The report uses LLMs to scan and filter the information from various sources, such as text, audio, or video, and extract the key signals, indicators, and drivers of change. The report also uses LLMs to categorize and label the trends according to various criteria, such as type, impact, duration, and uncertainty.

  - Trend monitoring: The report uses LLMs to track and measure the changes and developments that occur in the trends, such as frequency, intensity, scope, and direction. The report also uses LLMs to update and refine the trends according to the new information and evidence that emerges.

  - Trend forecasting: The report uses LLMs to project and extrapolate the trends into the future, based on various scenarios, assumptions, and models. The report also uses LLMs to generate and evaluate the potential opportunities and threats that the trends may create for the business and society.

- Results and Findings: The report presents the results and findings of the trend analysis, based on the data collected, analyzed, and visualized, from various sources, related to the market, industry, target market, customer segment, and value proposition. The report identifies, monitors, and forecasts the following trends:

- The increasing awareness and demand for health and wellness products and services, which has increased by 20% in the past year, and is expected to increase by 30% in the next five years, across various regions, segments, and categories, and is driven by the COVID-19 pandemic, the aging population, and the wellness movement. This is a social and consumer trend, with a high impact and duration, and a low uncertainty. This trend creates the following opportunities and threats for the business and society:

    - Opportunities: The business can tap into a large and growing market, industry, and domain, that has a high demand and potential for personalized and adaptive fitness coaching, using LLMs, and that can improve the health and wellness of the customers and society, and help them achieve their fitness goals, in a customized and flexible way.

    - Threats: The business may face some competition and substitution, that may affect the attractiveness and profitability of the platform, such as other platforms that offer personalized and adaptive fitness coaching, using LLMs or other technologies, and that may offer better or cheaper solutions, products, or services.

- The advancement and innovation of technologies, such as artificial intelligence, natural language processing, and data science, which has improved by 50% in the past year, and is expected to improve by 100% in the next five years, across various domains, tasks, and applications, and is driven by the breakthroughs and discoveries, such as GPT-3, OpenAI Codex, and Replika. This is a technological and economic trend, with a high impact and duration, and a medium uncertainty. This trend creates the following opportunities and threats for the business and society:

    - Opportunities: The business can leverage the power and potential of LLMs, to generate and adapt high-quality, relevant, and engaging fitness content, across various levels, subjects, and modalities, and to explore and exploit the new possibilities, insights, and solutions that LLMs can provide, and experiment with new ways of interacting with LLMs, and create new value for the customers and society.

- Threats: The business may face some risks and uncertainties, that may affect the quality, reliability, and ethics of the LLMs, such as complexity, opacity, unpredictability, and vulnerability, and that may harm the reputation, trust, and credibility of the business.

○ The ethical, legal, and social challenges and controversies, such as privacy, security, bias, and accountability, which has increased by 30% in the past year, and is expected to increase by 40% in the next five years, across various sectors, industries, and domains, and is driven by the incidents and scandals, such as Cambridge Analytica, Facial Recognition, and Deepfakes. This is a political and environmental trend, with a medium impact and duration, and a high uncertainty. This trend creates the following opportunities and threats for the business and society:

- Opportunities: The business can differentiate itself from the competitors, and build a loyal and engaged customer base and community, by ensuring the quality, reliability, and ethics of the LLMs, and by complying with the standards, guidelines, regulations, and audits of the education sector and society, and by addressing and resolving the ethical, legal, and social challenges and controversies, that may arise from the LLMs.
- Threats: The business may face some challenges and controversies, that may affect the acceptance and adoption of the LLMs, such as privacy, security, bias, and accountability, and that may trigger some backlash, resistance, and regulation from the customers, competitors, and stakeholders.

- Recommendations and Action Plans: The report provides some recommendations and action plans for the future, based on the results and findings of the trend analysis, and the potential opportunities and threats that the trends may create for the business and society. The report recommends and suggests the following steps and strategies:
  - Create and launch a platform that uses LLMs to provide personalized and adaptive fitness coaching, for young adults and fitness enthusiasts, based on their goals, preferences, and performance, and to follow some steps and strategies, such as:
    - Define the target market, customer segments, and value proposition.
    - Conduct market research and trend analysis to validate the assumptions and hypotheses, and to measure the performance and impact.
    - Develop a prototype or a minimum viable product (MVP) of the platform, and test it with the potential customers and users, and collect feedback and data.
    - Fine-tune, customize, and optimize the LLMs for the specific domain, task, and audience, and ensure their quality, reliability, and ethics.
    - Design a clear and sustainable business model and revenue stream, and secure funding and resources for the platform.
    - Launch and market the platform, and build a loyal and engaged customer base and community.
    - Monitor and evaluate the platform, and iterate and improve the solution, product, or service, based on the feedback and data collected.
  - Anticipate and prepare for the future, by creating and exploring various possible and plausible futures that may occur in the market, industry, and society, based on the trends, uncertainties, and events, and by imagining and

testing how the business would perform and survive in different situations and environments. The report also suggests some scenario planning methods and techniques, such as scenario matrix, scenario narratives, scenario simulations, scenario games, and more.

- ○ Create and shape the future, by influencing and driving the changes and developments that the business wants to see and achieve in the market, industry, and society, based on the vision, mission, and goals of the business, and by creating and delivering value and benefit for the customers and society. The report also suggests some innovation and disruption methods and techniques, such as brainstorming, mind mapping, ideation, prototyping, testing, validation, and more.

IN THIS CHAPTER, YOU have learned how to discover and seize the untapped potential and emerging trends of LLM entrepreneurship, such as new markets, industries, and domains, new customer needs and preferences, new business models and revenue streams, new partnerships and collaborations, and new innovations and breakthroughs.

You have also learned how to use LLMs for market research, trend analysis, opportunity identification, and scenario planning. You have also seen some examples and predictions of the future of LLM entrepreneurship, and how you can be part of it.

I hope that this chapter has inspired and motivated you to become a successful LLM entrepreneur, and to leverage the power of LLMs to create value for your customers and society.

I also hope that this chapter has provided you with some useful and practical tools and techniques, as well as some exercises and case studies, to help you practice and apply what you have learned, and to test and improve your skills and knowledge of LLM entrepreneurship.

Thank you for reading this chapter, and I hope you enjoyed it. ☺

Conclusion: The LLM Advantage

We have come to the end of our journey exploring the exciting world of LLM entrepreneurship. In this book, you learned what LLMs are and how they are revolutionizing business and innovation in the 21st century.

You discovered how LLMs can help entrepreneurs like you generate ideas, validate assumptions, build products, attract customers, measure results, and improve businesses across every industry. You also learned practical frameworks and methodologies for planning and executing LLM-powered business ventures, overcoming obstacles, and seizing emerging opportunities.

Along the way, we covered a wide range of topics, from the basics of how LLMs work to real-world case studies of companies using LLMs successfully. You got to try out LLMs yourself through hands-on exercises. And you learned key lessons from pioneers and experts applying LLMs in diverse domains.

I hope this book provided you with a comprehensive yet accessible introduction to leveraging the power of language, logic, and math models for your business success. My goal was to equip you with the knowledge and skills to become an LLM entrepreneur, regardless of your technical background.

At this point, you should have a clear understanding of:

- What LLMs are and how they generate, comprehend, and interact with natural language

- The impact of LLMs on business activities like product development, marketing, customer service, operations, and more

- How to cultivate an LLM entrepreneur mindset of curiosity, creativity, critical thinking, experimentation, and adaptation

- Practical techniques to use LLMs for ideation, assumption validation, prototyping, testing, product building, customer acquisition, results measurement, and business improvement

- A methodology to plan and execute LLM-based business ventures using the Lean Startup approach of build-measure-learn

- Ways to address the technical, ethical, legal, social, and environmental challenges of LLM entrepreneurship

- How to identify emerging LLM opportunities through market research, trend analysis, and scenario planning

You should also have hands-on experience interacting with LLMs, and knowledge of real-world examples of companies effectively leveraging LLMs.

The LLM revolution is just getting started. As LLMs continue advancing rapidly, they will open up more possibilities that we cannot even imagine today. There will be challenges as well, which responsible LLM entrepreneurs like you can help address.

By taking the time to learn about LLMs now, you have the knowledge and foresight to ride this wave of innovation. I hope the concepts, examples, and exercises in this book will serve you well on your journey to harness the power of LLMs for your business success.

As an early explorer of the LLM frontier, you have the opportunity to create substantial value for customers and society. The world needs entrepreneurs like you who approach LLMs thoughtfully and ethically.

I wish you the very best as you embark on your LLM-powered business ventures. Stay curious, creative, and human-centered. Use the LLM advantage wisely and make a positive impact. The future is yours to shape.

Onward!

Did you love *The LLM Advantage: How to Unlock the Power of Language Models for Business Success*? Then you should read *Entrepreneurship and Dharma : Gita Inspired Insights*[1] by ASISH DASH!

Building a business is hard work, but it's even harder if you're not passionate about what you're doing. That's why the Gita's teachings on Dharma are so relevant to entrepreneurship. Dharma is all about finding your purpose and living your life in a way that aligns with your values. When you can apply this principle to your work, you'll find that building a business becomes a lot more meaningful and fulfilling.

Of course, finding your purpose is easier said than done. That's why the Gita also teaches us the importance of self-reflection and introspection. By taking the time to reflect on our values and motivations, we can gain a better understanding of what drives us and what we want to achieve. This can help us make better decisions in our businesses and create a more authentic and purpose-driven brand.

1. https://books2read.com/u/3Jn0kP

2. https://books2read.com/u/3Jn0kP

Another key lesson from the Gita is the importance of ethical leadership. In today's world, where we see so many examples of unethical behavior in business, it's more important than ever to lead with integrity and moral courage. By being transparent, accountable, and socially responsible, we can build businesses that not only create wealth but also contribute to the greater good.

Ultimately, the principles of Business Entrepreneurship from the Gita and the rules of Dharma remind us that business is not just about making money. It's about creating something that has a positive impact on the world, and that aligns with our deepest values and aspirations. When we approach business in this way, we can find a sense of purpose and fulfillment that goes beyond mere financial success.

Read more at https://in.linkedin.com/in/dashasish.

Also by ASISH DASH

The Shy Entrepreneur
Insights From A Shy Entrepreneur
Insights from a Shy Entrepreneur : Turning Slowdown into Opportunity

Standalone
Entrepreneurship and Dharma : Gita Inspired Insights
The LLM Advantage: How to Unlock the Power of Language Models for
Business Success

Watch for more at https://in.linkedin.com/in/dashasish.

About the Author

Asish Dash, is the Founder of Grazing Minds - the fastest growing sustainable consulting edtech platform.

Asish defines himself as 3E. (Engineer, Economist and Entrepreneur) an alumnus of world's Top 10 university and various other institutes.

Frugality in business, is his passion and so is creating low cost self sustaining business models.He loves talking, studying and decoding business models and innovation around it.

After 3 successful startups, He is all into sharing information. He believes writing books is one way in which he can connect to my audiences apart from the consulting he does on LinkedIn.

Though some of his opinions may be termed as brash and opinionated - but he says, he is not here to appease any corporations or lobbies!!

Read more at https://in.linkedin.com/in/dashasish.

About the Publisher

Grazing Minds publishing is the subsidiary of Grazing Minds Research and Consulting, the knowledge arm founded by serial entrepreneur Asish Dash. It provides consulting and edtech services in the field of management, finance, banking, logistics and hospitality.

Milton Keynes UK
Ingram Content Group UK Ltd.
UKHW040717201123
432908UK00002B/441